Secrets of
Hiring
Top Talent

Daniel Abramson, CTS
President, **Staff**Dynamics®

Library of Congress Cataloging-in-Publication Data
on file with the Publisher

ISBN 1-59196-926-3

Printed in the United States of America by
Instantpublisher.com.

Dedication

The partnership, help, caring, honest feedback, fun and support that are represented by a loving family are a treasure that has worth beyond all calculation.

Lisa, my wife, Catherine and Caroline, my daughters, you are the best people in the world!

This book is dedicated to you.

Secrets of Hiring
Top Talent

Contents

Chapter One

Read This Book!

This book is about attracting, recruiting, hiring and retaining good people for your company. This is a topic that has become the most important competitive issue facing business today, and will remain so for at least the next ten years.

Here are four critical trends that underscore why this is so:

1. **Good people are already difficult to recruit and hire, and the demographics say that it's going to get a lot harder before it gets easier.** The following chart, based on US Bureau of Labor Statistics

population and jobs data, illustrates what's going to be happening through the year 2010:

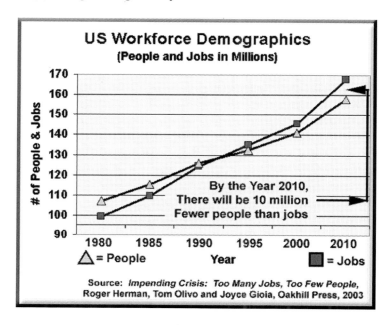

This chart shows that by the year 2010, there will be 10 million fewer skilled people than jobs in the US economy. Check it again -- that's fewer PEOPLE than JOBS – 10 million jobs that will go unfilled.

How did that come to pass? It happened because of the life-style choices made by the Baby-Boom generation -- those people who were born between 1946 and 1964, are now in their 40's, 50's and 60's, and are getting ready to leave the workforce in sizeable quantities. The Baby-Boom generation did not have large enough families to replace their own numbers in the workforce, and those shortfalls are catching up with us now.

2. **The continuing shift from a manufacturing- to a services-based economy means that the hiring**

requirements of most companies are changing dramatically. What used to be a fairly straightforward process – hiring – has become much more challenging, requiring new criteria and methods as employee compatibility with team members and corporate culture become increasingly essential to the mission of creating smooth work-flow processes and customer satisfaction. For the most part, these changes in job requirements have not been addressed in the hiring processes that companies currently use. Modern companies need people who can wear multiple hats, and who have the flexibility and character to adapt quickly and ethically to changing conditions. In particular, they need people who have the ability to communicate effectively with customers, and who work well with their peers, while floating in an ocean of change. Yet the criteria by which we evaluate candidates continue to focus almost exclusively on discrete skills and experience, ignoring the personality attributes and character traits that are the much more relevant indicators of long-term candidate success.

3. **Cost factors and short-term business downturns have "leaned-out" most companies to the point where their staffing levels are barely sufficient to handle current workloads.** Because companies are so lean and their structures are so flat, their employees are multi-tasking almost to the point of exhaustion, and backup bench strength for key positions is virtually nonexistent. As the economy rebounds, these corporations will be hard pressed to accommodate even small increases in demand for their products and services, and many will find themselves caught in a hiring gridlock where they cannot expand quickly enough to satisfy the needs of their customers.

4. **Despite soft hiring activity in some markets, voluntary turnover is running at a high level – just under 20% annually across all industries in the US.**

This level of turnover reflects pent-up frustration among employees, many of whom are going to leave their current employers in even greater numbers as economic conditions improve. This impulse to change jobs has been exacerbated in recent years because of corporate downsizing – employees are no longer loyal to companies that they feel have not shown loyalty to them. Given the ongoing trend toward too many jobs and too few people, these employees will have plenty of options when they decide it's time to leave.

These factors -- too many jobs, changing requirements and outmoded practices, hiring gridlock and turnover – have converged to create a situation where the most important job of managers is hiring, and where retaining their existing employees follows hiring as a close second place.

Who am I to be saying these things to you? My name is Daniel Abramson, and I am President of **StaffDynamics®**, a Washington, DC-based consulting firm, as well as a national speaker on workforce performance issues.

My consulting firm provides recruiting, employee assess-ment, training, briefing and executive coaching services to companies of all sizes. If you are reading this book, you may well have participated with me in a seminar sponsored by your company, or perhaps you have attended one on your own.

For almost 25 years, I have been involved in all aspects of recruiting, hiring and retaining employees. I have worked in sales management in the health care and consumer products industries, as an owner of a recruiting business, as president of a large search and staffing firm, and now as founder of a workforce consulting firm. Along the way, I've hired a lot of people, and have been involved in thousands of recruiting and hiring transactions. I have also managed and fired people, and have lost a few good ones. Like many managers, I've always been on the lookout for better methods. What makes my experience different from most is that my combined roles on "both sides of the desk" as a corporate manager and a search and staffing industry practitioner and executive have given me a unique perspective. That perspective has broadened my viewpoint and fueled my commitment to define and document a more effective process for attracting, recruiting, hiring and retaining good people.

The information presented here is not the result of a single flash of insight. Rather, I learned it the old fashioned way: through trial and error, adjustments and determined retrials -- and in conversations with hundreds of managers and executives -- over time.

Here's what we'll be addressing in this book:

❖ In **Chapter Two,** we'll explore the widespread imbalance between the criteria we use when we hire candidates and the reasons we give when we fire them. The chapter will demonstrate the downsides of this imbalance, and then go on to point the way for its repair.

❖ In **Chapter Three,** we'll investigate employee turnover. We'll learn how widespread the turnover problem is and how much it costs. We'll also look at what to do when it happens to your company, and we'll take a beginning stab at methods for preventing it. As you examine the numbers on turnover, I think you'll gain a new appreciation for how significant a problem it really is.

❖ **Chapter Four** lists 10.5 hiring blunders that you should avoid at all costs. Included are primers, pointers and checklists that you can use to make sure those blunders don't happen on your watch.

❖ **Chapter Five** presents a concrete method for factoring personality traits into the hiring and management mix.

It introduces "DISC theory" and the "DISC Personality Survey," two powerful tools for confirming your impressions and mapping your candidates' (or employees') potential. After showing how DISC can be integrated into the candidate selection process, the chapter concludes with several examples of how it can be used to improve performance, as a selling tool, and in business communications and crisis management.

◈ **Chapter Six** lays out a proven 10-step hiring process which meets the standards of balance introduced in Chapter Two, incorporates the personality tools from Chapter Five, and avoids the blunders included in Chapter Four. This chapter provides detailed instructions, pointers, evaluation checklists, rules of thumb and scripts for implementing those ten hiring steps.

◈ **Chapter Seven** states that the real wealth of a company is based on the knowledge of its employees, and imparts eight proven strategies you can use to stabilize your organization and nurture the growth of your employees.

◈ **Chapter Eight** summarizes the high points of the first seven chapters, and makes specific action recommendations for each of them.

What this book is *not* about is theory, jargon, buzzwords and whimsy. Rather, it's designed to be practical, doable and realistic. The methods that are presented here are approaches that work. The checklists, pointers and scripts that are included have real-life application.

Because of the practical, doable and realistic nature of this material, it lends itself well to action. To facilitate that process further, all chapters except this one and the last one have a page at the end entitled, "Chapter Take-Aways." The purpose of these pages is to encourage to you to convert what you've learned into action by writing down specific checklist items you want to pursue. Having made the commitment to provide this material to you, I'm asking for your commitment in return. Use the Chapter Take-Aways.

You will notice one or two terms in this book that you may not have heard before – most notably, "Hiring Manager." "Hiring Manager" has a simple definition: it's any Manager who has occasion to Hire.

So if you are -- or plan to be -- or want to be -- or used to be -- or may be -- or know -- a Hiring Manager, read on. This book is for you. Read it with the knowledge that every time the phrase, "Hiring Manager," appears, it's my reminder to you that **Hiring Is Your Most Important Job.**

Chapter Two

We Hire For Skills, Fire for Personality

When it comes to recruiting and hiring, North American businesspeople are a skills-oriented culture.

To demonstrate this for yourself, all you have to do is browse Monster, Hot Jobs, Career Builder or most other of the many on-line Job Boards, and count the number of words focused on skills, experience and knowledge needed. Now compare that total to the number of words used to describe other types of requirements, like attitude, ability to learn, team orientation, character and work ethic, in those same postings. I'm sure that on any given day, you'll find the ratio to be about 85%-15% (or almost 6:1) in favor of skills, experience and knowledge needed over the other factors.

Think about it for a second . . . or better yet, think about it while viewing the following chart:

85%	15%
• **Technical skills** • **Background and experience**	• **Personality Attributes** • **Attitude** • **Ability to Learn** • **Chemistry and "Fit"** • **Team Orientation** • **Character** • **Work Ethic**

Now ask yourself this question: "Which list can I afford to overlook in recruiting, identifying and selecting the people I want to have working for me?"

Follow up by asking yourself another question as well: "Which list would I emphasize and which one would I exclude if I want the people I hire to be long-term players on my team, in my department or company?"

In case you don't yet see this ratio as a potential problem, think about it again, while looking at the following graphic:

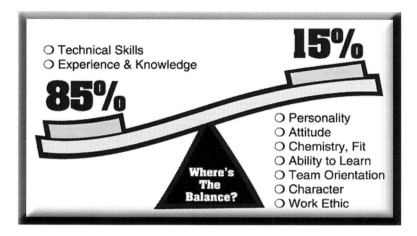

As you can see, the focus on skills, experience and knowledge far outweighs the concern for attitude, ability to learn, character, chemistry and fit, team and work ethic. It's almost as if those items are not important. In my experience, this seesaw is not a fantasy graph -- it depicts a pattern of hiring practices that is all too prevalent, and all too real, throughout the culture of North American business. Quite simply, it represents the way most of us tend to hire, most of the time. And given this reality, we have to wonder how often we miss something very critical when making our hiring decisions. Like the picture says, we need to ask, "Where's the balance?"

But let's be fair. You WILL find some reference to personality, character, work ethic and attitude, etc., in recruiting ads and job specifications. And, as many people might argue, the job ad or spec may not really the proper vehicle for addressing these types of criteria, anyway. Nonetheless, if you ever have occasion to observe and evaluate the overall pattern of hiring practices and concerns in a large number of companies over a period of a number of years, as I have, you will note that technical skill, knowledge and experience factors most often DO take precedence over "the other stuff." You will no doubt conclude that this pattern of hiring makes us all a little less able to succeed as managers, a little less equipped to do our jobs in spotting, recruiting and hiring the best possible candidates for the positions we need to fill.

Now For the Bad News

I think that almost everyone would agree with me that bad hiring can be the catalyst for a chain of cause-and-effect reactions that have major implications for every level of a business and all industries. Here is an illustration of how a pattern of hiring that "misses something important" can affect every aspect of your company: from the people being hired, to their co-workers, to the people doing the hiring, to the company's internal and external Customers, to departmental and corporate performance and profits, to the company's overall value in the marketplace:

(facing page)

The Bad Hiring Reaction Chain		
(When Key Factors Are Overlooked)		
The People Hired	⬇	• They may have the skill, but not the will, to do their jobs. • They may not be able to work with team members. • They may be over-stressed by the job functions assigned to them. • They may be fired, or cause others to leave.
Their Fellow Employees or Team Members	⬇	• They will not be able to rely on the new hires. • They'll be distracted by the amount of time and effort it takes to work with the new hires. • Their morale, commitment to goals and shared sense of mission will suffer as a result.
Depart-mental Perfor-mance	⬇	• The department will get behind schedule and go over budget. • The department's ability to function smoothly will be hampered.

(continued)

13

The Bad Hiring Reaction Chain
(When Key Factors Are Overlooked)

Internal Customers	⬇	• Others who depend on the services of the department or team will feel the impact. • Their performance will also be compromised.
Departmental Managers and Executives	⬇	• Departmental Managers and Executives will be forced to spend too much time as "referees," correcting mistakes and reassigning tasks. • Their efforts at damage control will eventually erode their credibility.
External Customers	⬇	• Inappropriate hires spell Customer dissatisfaction, and a further drain on resources. • Dissatisfied Customers will eventually bolt.

(continued)

The Bad Hiring Reaction Chain
(When Key Factors Are Overlooked)

Corporate Perfor- mance	⬇	• Lost External Customers slow revenues and impede growth. • Unhappy Internal Customers lower productivity. • These factors combine to undermine profits.
Corporate Market Share	⬇	• Lost revenues result in shrinking market share, dwindling corporate clout and diminished name recognition.
Corporate Market Equity	⬇ ═	• As productivity, revenues, profits, market share and name recognition continue to decline, so will the overall value of the business.

While the example shown above may seem a little extreme, remember that I'm talking about a *pattern of hiring practice*, here, not the hiring of just one individual. Even with the best tools and processes at our disposal, we all can, and will, make a hiring mistake from time to time. Those mistakes, when discovered early enough, can usually be corrected without doing lasting damage. However, when an inappropriate hiring pattern is repeated over and over, and that pattern affects a significant percentage of the employees in a company, department or team, regardless of its size, the results can be as dire as the illustration describes. The best case is that those hiring practices will hold an otherwise good enterprise back. Worst case – and especially if they are combined with the onset of clever and competent competition and unfriendly market conditions – those practices will contribute to the enterprise's demise.

Some Good News

The good news in all of this is that the way we hire is only a pattern of behavior, a process that can be mastered and modified. Even more important, most of what will be presented here can be done by you, personally, working at the departmental or team level – with no special authorization required from above. The costs of recruiting, hiring and retaining right are very minimal – they are miniscule, in fact, when compared with the costs of bad hiring. Further, the steps that are designed to make the needed changes in hiring behavior are easy to comprehend and implement.

As I stated in Chapter One, everything written here is designed to be practical, doable and realistic. You will not be asked to learn new jargon or engage in activities that are beyond your capabilities and comfort level. Rather, you'll be introduced to some basic principles and findings from the behavioral sciences, along with best hiring practices derived from nearly two decades in the staffing industry. These principles, findings and practices have been applied here in a form that will be readily recognizable from your day-to-day experiences as a Manager. If you are new to hiring and management, you will still be familiar with most of what is being presented, from your life experiences as a student, job candidate and employee.

Hard Skills, Soft Skills

To begin the process of keeping things simple, let's redefine some terms. Up to now, I've been describing two types of attributes that help us determine which

Candidates we should hire. I've used phrases like, "technical skills, knowledge and experience," on the one hand, and "the other stuff" on the other.

Let's take our first step toward changing our behavior by giving those phrases some better labels. Let's call them "Hard Skills" and "Soft Skills." By agreeing to use these labels, we accomplish two very useful objectives:

1. **We level the playing field. Now both types of attributes are called "skills" – there's no hierarchy; they're just different kinds of skills. We have a much better chance of addressing both on an equal footing.**

2. **The "handles" we've created are easy to remember and understand. So we've got a more solid foundation upon which to build.**

Using the new labels, things get simpler. The seesaw chart is easier to read:

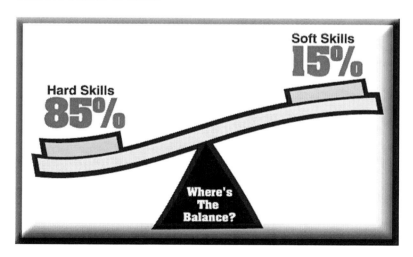

Yet its message is still the same. All too often when hiring, we focus on Hard Skills while sacrificing Soft Skills. The way we hire tells us a great deal about what the candidate is capable of doing, a tiny bit about what he or she will do, and almost zero about how he or she compares with our other employees, will fit into our work style, mesh with our team, handle deadlines and pressure, and relate to the specifics of his or her role on the job.

The Reverse is True at Termination

As much as we tend when hiring to emphasize Hard Skills over Soft Skills, the reverse is true when it comes time to fire someone. When the "firing clock" starts ticking, Hard Skills and Soft Skills make a dramatic switcheroo. Having hired for skills, we now tend to fire for personality. While it is true that a few people are terminated because their Hard Skills do not stand up under the pressure and scrutiny of the initial work experience, most people are terminated for Soft-Skill reasons, for reasons having to do with personality.

To help illustrate this from the perspective of your own reality, I'd like to ask you to complete the following exercise. Take a look at the table below and check off those "Reasons For Firing" which ring a bell in your personal experience. Do so by marking the "Sounds Familiar" boxes that are positioned on the left-hand side of the table:

(facing page)

Sounds Familiar	Reason for Firing	Type of Skill	
❏	Didn't have the skills and background to perform the critical tasks.	❏ Hard	❏ Soft
❏	Job specifications changed. Could not or would not learn new critical tasks.	❏ Hard	❏ Soft
❏	Didn't know how to use _____ (software, system, technology or procedure) as well as advertised.	❏ Hard	❏ Soft
❏	Couldn't get along with other department members.	❏ Hard	❏ Soft
❏	Always late, disorganized, bored – too much of a "dreamer" for this job.	❏ Hard	❏ Soft
❏	Blew a critical assignment and made no effort to fix it. Tried to blame others.	❏ Hard	❏ Soft
❏	Difficult to deal with. Would not take input. Lousy listener.	❏ Hard	❏ Soft
❏	Too many complaints about shoddy work.	❏ Hard	❏ Soft

For the ones you've checked as "Familiar," now go back through and indicate which are Hard Skills and which are Soft Skills by checking the appropriate boxes to the right of the table. The more analytical folks among us may contend that some of the items listed involve above both types of Skills -- Hard and Soft. Well, OK -- everything's always got some shades of gray, but bear with me. If you are like most people, you will probably select five or more of the reasons listed and classify the majority of them as involving Soft Skills. If you selected all eight Reasons for Firing as sounding familiar, your chart will look something like this:

Sounds Familiar	Reason for Firing	Type of Skill	
☑	Didn't have the skills and background to perform the critical tasks.	☑ Hard	☐ Soft
☑	Job specifications changed. Couldn't / wouldn't learn new critical tasks.	☐ Hard	☑ Soft
☑	Didn't know how to use _____ (software or system) as well as advertised.	☑ Hard	☐ Soft
☑	Couldn't get along with other department members.	☐ Hard	☑ Soft
☑	Always late, disorganized, bored – too much of a "dreamer" for this job.	☐ Hard	☑ Soft
☑	Blew a critical assignment and made no effort to fix it. Tried to blame others.	☐ Hard	☑ Soft
☑	Difficult to deal with. Would not take input. Lousy listener.	☐ Hard	☑ Soft
☑	Too many complaints about shoddy work.	☐ Hard	☑ Soft

You'll notice that most of the items checked are Soft Skills – 6 of 8 in our example, or 75% for Soft-Skill Reasons, versus 25% for Hard-Skill Reasons. In the real world of work, my experience is that that ratio is closer to 85 to 15, Soft-Skill Reasons to Hard-Skill Reasons. So the relationship between the two kinds of skills looks just like our original seesaw graph, only with the emphasis reversed:

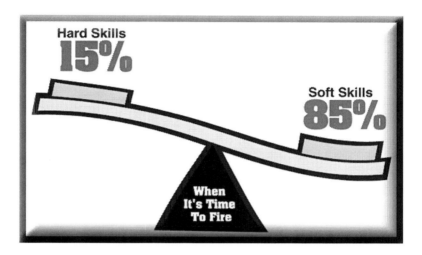

Why is it that people are six times more likely to be fired for their Soft Skills than for their Hard Skills? It's because while their Hard Skills define their technical and experiential capabilities, their Soft Skills – i.e., their personality characteristics -- determine their level of success. In other words, Hard Skills show what a person Can Do, while Soft Skills indicate what that person Will Do.

Granted, these Soft-Skill personality characteristics are not easily visible to the naked eye during the recruiting and hiring process. It's much easier to unearth the number of years of experience a person has with a certain industrial procedure or programming language than to determine whether that person's Soft Skills mean that he or she will be a solid employee who will consistently make a high-quality contribution. Yet it is those Soft Skills -- those more elusive personality factors -- that will set that person's style, tone and attitude as he or she makes (or breaks) his or her way through your business.

Style, tone and attitude are very important, as are Behavior, Attitude and Work Ethic (BAW) and Attitude, Interest and Motivation (AIM). Each of those catchphrases and acronyms has a slightly different way of capturing some of what we're looking for when we explore the personality factors that make up a person's character. With Attitude as their common denominator, they represent values and patterns of behavior that are deeply rooted within all of us long before we enter the workplace. Once we've become adults, these characteristics don't change much – they just are. As the saying goes, "You can teach Skills, but not Attitude." Since we can't do much to change a person's Soft Skills, it's our job as Hiring Managers to identify and use them during the selection process as we make our hiring decisions.

The Hiring Process Holds the Keys

If it ever comes to pass that you have to fire someone you once hired (and it probably will), you will experience two, very strong emotions. First, whether the person being let go is gracious or not as he or she exits your company, you will probably end up wishing you'd never hired him or her in the first place. This is not just because of his or her attitude, or your guilt, anger or frustration during the termination, but also because of all the time you put into developing him or her – with nothing to show for it except the requirement to start over. Second, as you think back and recognize some of the early-warning signals you missed or ignored from this person during your initial hiring meetings with him or her, you will feel a compelling desire to capture those signals in your memory for all time, and to do all in your power to make sure you *never make those same mistakes again!*

Your impulse to avoid repeating the same mistakes in the future is right on target. But achieving your goal is likely to require more than a few, minor adjustments. If you really want to eliminate a pattern of hiring mistakes, your challenge will be to broaden your focus beyond the scope of the signals you saw and ignored. Your task will be to develop a system or process of hiring that brings all of the critical factors into account, not just a few new techniques.

This is not to say that your efforts to improve your personal hiring, interviewing and listening skills will not bear fruit. They will, and for that reason we'll include traps to avoid in Chapter Four – *Hiring Blunders We All Have Made*, and hiring and interviewing tips in Chapter 6 – *Hiring Winners*. But to make your hiring practices as good as your hopes and goals for your department or team, and to make sure they take a form that can be used again and again, you'll need to master and modify the *process that generated the information* that led you to your hiring decisions, not just the specific miscues that you can recall.

In short, your task will be to put a hiring process in place that presents you with the information you'll need to make good hiring decisions all of the time.

If your hiring process is right, you'll hire right. If your process is wrong and you make a good hire, that's luck. You beat the odds this time, but those odds will catch up with you next time. If the process is right and you hire wrong, you've simply made a mistake. If you have a good process and you make a good hire, you'll add a great employee to your staff. You'll also have the tools in place to hire consistently right in the future.

This is a critical idea, so let me say it again.

> *Your hiring process*
> *Holds the keys*
> *To hiring right.*

Revisiting the Seesaw

Having established the importance of the hiring process, let's take another look at our two seesaw graphs, this time comparing them side-by-side:

(see facing page)

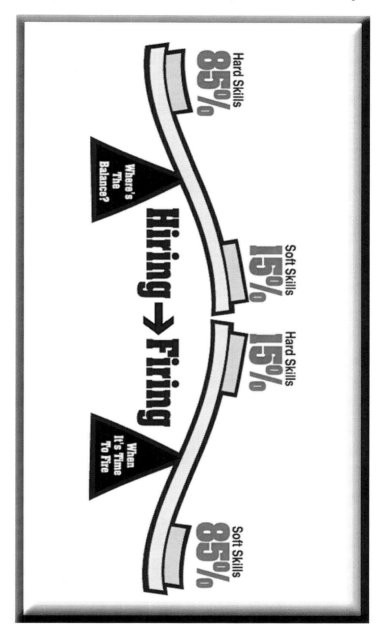

When we view these two graphs from the point of view of the hiring process they represent, their central contradiction comes into sharper focus. The criteria we use to hire people are very different from the criteria we use to retain or terminate them. The people we hire gain entry into our companies based on their Hard Skills, and too many of those same people get shown the door based on their Soft Skills. If our objective is to hire people who can become long-term contributors, then it is apparent that our hiring processes tend to encourage us to ignore critical factors in making the decisions that create those hires.

In fact, when you look at the seesaw graphs this way, it seems as if our hiring processes are designed to *generate* turnover, rather than reduce it. We'll pick up on this idea again, when we tackle turnover and retention in Chapters Three and Seven.

What We Are Saying

In case there's any question, the fact that we hire for skills and fire for personality is not a good thing. It may be a practice that is based on a Darwinian notion of natural selection, but it is also the line of least resistance that results in too many bad hires. It's a process that needs to be redesigned, to paraphrase one Dr. Stephen Covey's *Seven Habits of Highly Effective People,* with a better outcome in mind. If our goal is to build strong organizations and highly functional teams, then hiring for skills and firing for personality is not the way to do it.

The Hiring / Firing Time Line

Another way to view the seesaw chart is by looking at the way our concerns about our new employees evolve over time. Take a look at the revised chart below, which has a time line added at the bottom:

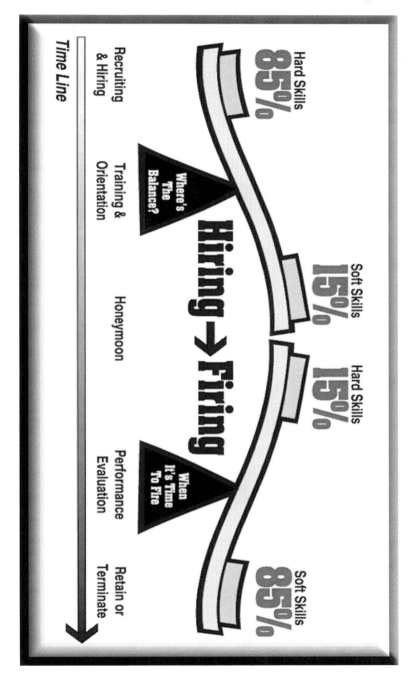

Since the average time from hire to termination of a bad-hire new employee across all mid-level job roles ranges from seven to eight months, the total duration of the time line shown above is averaged at 7½ months. The timeline is broken into five segments, or phases, each of which is approximately 1 ½ months (or 45 days) long.

Here's how the phases play out:

Phase	What's Going On
I. Recruiting & Hiring **Days # 1 – 45** **Total Elapsed Time: 1½ months**	• New employees are still basking in the glow of the new job. • Most co-workers are taking a "hands-off" attitude. • Soft-Skill mistakes are written off as "to be expected from a brand-new employee." • Little is known yet about the new employees' Hard Skills beyond what was on their resumes.
II. Training & Orientation **Days # 46 – 90** **Total Elapsed Time: 3 months**	• New employees are expected to perform at a low level, but are given lots of latitude. • If Hard Skills are weaker than originally thought, it is usually the trainer who sees the signs first, and additional training or learning assignments are given.

Phase	What's Going On
III. Honey-moon **Days #** **91 – 135** **Total Elapsed Time: 4½ months**	• By now, the new employees have taken on full duties and performance responsibilities, but are still given some slack if they fail to perform to standard. • If Hard Skills are lacking, the group will tend to forgive them based on the employees' Soft Skills. • The focus is clearly changing from Hard to Soft Skills, and the Honeymoon will soon be over.
IV. Perfor-mance Evaluation **Days #** **136 – 180** **Total Elapsed Time: 6 months**	• As more time passes, new employees either get assimilated into their new jobs or the group loses patience with them. • Hard Skills are now assumed. • Group focus is now almost entirely on Soft Skills – if they are absent, the "firing clock" starts ticking. • Bad-hire new employees will receive negative feedback from bosses and peers every day -- formal warnings may also take place.
V. Retain or Terminate **Days #** **181 – 225** **Total Elapsed Time: 7½ months**	• After the six-month point, it's usually just a matter of days until bad-hire new employees are put on final notice. • A small fraction of them will turn themselves around. • These are the exception. Most bad-hire employees will not have the Soft Skills to succeed, and their employment will be terminated.

As you can see, concerns about new employees shift over time from Hard Skills to Soft Skills, from experience-driven Can-Do factors to personality-driven Will-Do factors. This change takes place because it is generally the Soft Skills that allow the team or department to go on with its work, providing the "grease" that enables it to function smoothly. Given the way the process works in most companies, you can see that it will take several months to discover and then document the fact that a new employee is a bad hire, and then even more time for the Manager to take the appropriate actions.

The View from 30,000 Feet

If you and I were in a spy plane cruising at 30,000 feet, and we could watch this pattern of hiring and firing unfold from that vantage point, we'd be blown away by what a TIME ROBBER it all seems to be. We would ask, "Why does it have to take so long to find out about the factors that really predict the overall performance of new employees?" We'd follow up with, "Why can't some of these concerns be addressed earlier in the process, especially before the hire takes place?"

We would then feel compelled to put forth the following proposal:

> **"Here's a way to save a HUGE amount of time and frustration when hiring. Let's design a hiring process that uncovers more of the critical information – regarding the Soft Skills as well as the Hard Skills -- up front, BEFORE the hiring decision is made."**

That's our task -- to modify our hiring processes so that they uncover and assess a potential employee's Hard Skills and Soft Skills BEFORE the hiring decision is made.

Balance Is Our Goal

As we embark on our mission of fixing our hiring practices, we'll seek the seesaw's guidance once again, using it as a benchmark by which to measure our progress. We'll know we're reaching our goal when our hiring chart looks a little more like this one:

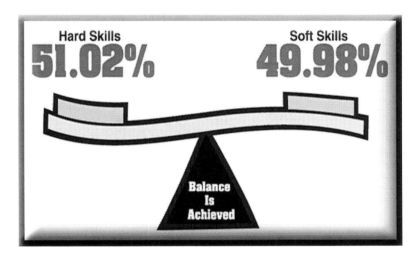

The exact percentages on each side of the balance point are not that important, as long as they're a lot closer to 50-50 than 85-15. What is important is that we install and use a balanced hiring process that brings all of the pivotal characteristics into play before the hiring decision is made.

By creating a balanced hiring process that takes all of the critical Hard and Soft Skills into account, we will recruit better people, make better hiring decisions and build better teams. We'll also save enormous amounts of time, frustration and money, enhancing our effectiveness as Hiring Managers.

	Chapter Take-Aways	
Item	**Idea, Issue or Action Item**	**Done / Noted**
1	We Hire for Skills and Fire for Personality – and this is not a Good Thing.	☐
2	Hard Skills = Technical and Experience Factors; Soft Skills = Character and Personality Factors.	☐
3	We need to modify our Hiring Process so that all of the critical factors – Soft and Hard Skills -- are discovered and assessed before the hire.	☐
4		☐
5		☐
6		☐
7		☐

Note: The purpose of this "Take-Away" page is to encourage you to summarize the key points of the materials you've read in this Chapter. To get the process started, I have listed three items that I feel are important, but this list is not exhaustive.

Take this opportunity to inventory what you've learned and crystallize what you want to implement before moving on.

Chapter Three

The Turnover Treadmill

I f you are ever asked to justify the merit of your mission to improve your company's hiring practices, you'll need to look no further than the numbers on turnover and its cost to US companies for a compelling response. These numbers are truly staggering. When you crunch the costs of turnover and multiply them by the number of people who change jobs voluntarily every year, what comes out is the astounding conclusion that turnover costs the U.S. economy almost TWO TRILLION DOLLARS PER YEAR.

Two trillion dollars – that's a "2" with twelve "zero's" after it. At two trillion dollars per year, this means that the annual cost of turnover is more than three times the annual budget of the U.S. Department of Defense, and is about equivalent to our yearly spend on health care.

How do we come up with such astronomical numbers? To set a baseline, here's what the U.S. Government says about turnover for 2003 (the last full year for which such numbers were available at the time this book was published):

➢ **According to the US Department of Labor, 36.9 % of all employees – or roughly 47,000,000 people -- *separated from their jobs for all reasons* during 2003.**

➢ **Those separation rates ran from over 70% in some industries to less than 20% in others.**

➢ **During that same period, 19.2% of all employees – or over 24,000,000 people – *terminated their employment voluntarily* in the US.**

➢ **These voluntary turnover rates ran from over 46% in higher-turnover industries to 11½% for lower-turnover segments.**

Think of it. 2003 was not exactly a banner year for the US economy. Rather, it was a year when one could safely assume that a large number of employees would continue to hunker down and wait for smoother sailing before moving to another company. And yet, over one-half of the people whose employment was terminated for any reason during that year – in round numbers, some 20% of the total workforce – left on their own accord. They were not fired or riffed or laid off or downsized or given a gold watch and a retirement dinner. They quit their jobs.

And this was in a down economy! This means that if your company is just average, one-fifth of your employees – i.e., 20% of your core workers, the ones you hoped would stay to help you shoulder the additional load caused by the cutbacks and freezes – tendered their resignations and went to work for someone else. If this is what the voluntary turnover numbers look like in a year with weak economic growth, how high are they going to go when the statistics come in for 2004, 2005 and beyond?

Expensive Consequences

These turnover percentages translate into very substantial costs. There are several formulas for calculating the cost of turnover, and those calculations can get very detailed. Workforce analysts Roger Herman, Tom Olivo and Joyce Gioia used a simplified version of the Bliss-Gately Tool in their recent book, *Impending Crisis: Too Many Jobs, Too Few People* (Oakdale Press, 2003), which we have summarized below. Their cost calculation model takes six factors into account, which we'll call "direct" turnover costs. For each of these factors, a percentage of salary is assessed that is added to the cost of keeping a position filled after it was vacated because of turnover. As shown in the chart below, the total "direct" cost of turnover using this method is 117.7% of salary:

Direct Turnover Costs	
Category	**% of Salary**
Costs Due to Employee Leaving	66.2%
Recruitment Costs (if no Search / Staffing firm or relocation are involved)	1.9%
Training Costs	18.2%
Lost Productivity Costs	31.2%
New Employee Costs	0.2%
Total Direct Costs	117.7%
Source: *Impending Crisis: Too Many Jobs, Too Few People* by Roger Herman, Tom Olivo and Joyce Gioia (Oakdale Press, 2003).	

All of these costs are incurred by a company *in addition to* the compensation for the person who is hired to replace the one who left the company. This means that, according to Herman, Olivo and Gioia, the total direct cost of replacing someone who leaves your company is *at least two times* that person's compensation.

Competitive Realities Mean Even Greater Costs

In reality, you can add at least another 100% to the cost of turnover over the 117.7% quoted above, as direct costs only tell part of the story. When you measure the cost of turnover in light of competitive realities, five additional factors need to be included in the equation. These factors involve costs that are less direct and more variable, but are nonetheless just as significant. Consider the following:

1. **Actual Recruitment Costs** for key skills will be much higher than the model shows. If a focused internal recruiting effort or a search firm is used, the full cost of that effort will add another 8.6% to 30% of salary. If relocation is also required to fill the position, that could add as much as another 20.6%

2. **Management Time** will be diverted from activities that generate revenues and optimize operations to the necessary activities of hiring and selecting the replacement. That lost time is worth 8 – 12% of compensation for each key person who must be replaced.

3. **Increased Compensation** will most likely be the result of having to go out into the marketplace to replace this position. In general, turnover-driven hires are brought into companies at 5 – 15% over what the incumbent was being paid.

4. **Lost Continuity and Customer Slippage** will inevitably result from turnover, particularly if the

company loses several key employees in a row. In today's tight organizations, each good employee plays a key role in providing needed services to your internal and/or external customers. Your key employees get better at their jobs by learning from the experience of doing them. When those employees leave, most of their knowledge leaves with them -- and so does some (or all) of the loyalty of those internal/external customers whom they served. While this consequence of turnover is easiest to quantify when a top salesperson leaves, it is just as real -- and just as costly -- when a non-sales employee leaves. When turnover is rampant, this kind of slippage can actually cause the demise of a company. As a cost factor, lost continuity and customer slippage is worth at least 20% of the employee's compensation, and in some cases a lot more than that.

5. **Opportunity Cost** -- Whether it takes the form of lost revenues or profits, new customers, product ideas or technologies not pursued, or business plans not perfected and implemented, the time and energy it takes Hiring Managers to replace key employees affects the long-term direction of the company as well as its day-to-day operations. Simply stated, if the Hiring Manager finds him- or herself to be continually in a firefighting mode because of a high rate of turnover, then the first thing that will suffer will be his or her ability to plan effectively for the future. Add another 10% of compensation to the cost of replacing each person lost.

Here's what these indirect variables add to the cost of turnover:

Total Turnover Costs		
Category	**% Range of Salary**	
	From	**To**
❖ **Total Direct Costs (from first chart)**	**117.7%**	**117.7%**
❖ **Plus Additional Indirect Costs:**		
• **Added Recruiting Costs**	**8.6%**	**30.0%**
• **Relocation Cost**	**0%**	**20.6%**
• **Diverted Management Time**	**8.0%**	**12.0%**
• **Increased Compensation**	**5.0%**	**15.0%**
• **Lost Continuity & Customer Slippage**	**20.0%**	**20.0%**
• **Opportunity Cost**	**10.0%**	**10.0%**
❖ **Total Indirect Costs**	**51.6%**	**107.6%**
Total Cost of Turnover	**169.3%**	**225.3%**

What do these numbers mean? For each key employee whom you as Hiring Manager retain in your organization during the next twelve months, your cost for that employee will be the amount of his or her compensation, only. For each key employee you lose and have to replace during the next twelve months, your cost for that loss and replacement will be between 2.69 and 3.25 times that employee's compensation – i.e., the employee's compensation plus that compensation times the percentage ranges shown in the table, above. As a general rule of thumb, remember the following:

Here's a final, sobering note on the cost of employee turnover. The US Bureau of Labor Statistics estimates that the average earnings of all US workers in all occupations were $17.41 per hour, or $36,213 per year, in 2003. If we take a very conservative view of the cost of turnover and multiply that compensation number by a factor of only 2.25, then the cost of losing and replacing each of those employees who left their jobs voluntarily was $81,479. According to the information from the US Department of Labor cited earlier in this chapter, over 24,000,000 people left their jobs voluntarily during 2003.

Now do the math. This means that the total loss-and-replacement cost to the US economy of those 24,000,000 people was, as we said at the beginning of this chapter, almost TWO TRILLION dollars. That's a HUGE cost for our nation's economy to bear!

The Turnover Treadmill

The current level of voluntary employee turnover is so high in the United States that, if a governmental agency were charged with the responsibility of achieving it, it would probably fail at the task. This agency would no doubt have to use mass marketing techniques and automated systems in order to reach its objectives. But even with those resources in place, it would not be able to compete with what the private sector has achieved through a set of hiring and management practices, assumptions and expectations that almost seem to be aimed at *generating* turnover rather than *preventing* it.

The result is that for many Hiring Managers, the process of hiring, then losing, key employees -- only to re-hire and then to lose them again -- is a treadmill that never stops. Indeed, it is a treadmill where the controls are locked up at top speed and where there is no visible means of escape.

If the condition I'm describing applied to turnover of marginal hires, only, then maybe we could find a way to mentally write off its vast annual cost. We could make the argument that many of those people wouldn't be so sorely missed, after all, and that companies could get along better without them. But this is not the case. The 20% voluntary turnover rate represents those people that the average company loses every year who are part of its core group – i.e., those the company wants to keep. And if a company loses one-fifth of its core employees every year, this means that the average company turns over its *entire core staff every five years!*

Clearly, this is NOT the way to develop a company's human capital asset to its fullest potential. And just as clearly, voluntary employee turnover is an area where there is an abundance of room – and just as hefty a measure of need – for improvement.

Why Employees Leave

There are so many studies on what causes employee turnover that it is impossible to sift through them all. While a great deal has recently been made of the fact that employees in general are less loyal to companies because so many corporations have shown little loyalty to their employees over the past decade or so, this is an abstract concept that does little to inform the Hiring Manager on how to proceed.

The following list of eleven top reasons why employees leave should be more practical, in that it cross-references the exit interview findings of Human Resources specialists with the most common reasons for leaving encountered by Search and Staffing professionals, both of whom invest a significant amount of time speaking with employees about these issues. As a beginning step in separating those reasons that can be addressed by Hiring Managers from those that cannot, it is organized into four, general categories of response:

#	Category / Reason
Reasons Why Employees Leave	
I.	**Management Factors:** 1. Conflicts with Supervisor / Management Philosophy 2. Intolerable Work Environment / Inflexible Rules 3. High Staff or Management Turnover 4. Inadequate Communications / Feel Isolated
II.	**Performance Factors:** 5. Unclear, Dramatically- or Rapidly- Changing Job Duties 6. Lack of Training
III.	**Motivational Factors:** 7. Lack of Challenge / No Career Path / Fear of Obsolescence 8. Lack of Recognition & Reward, Incentives
IV.	**Environmental Factors:** 9. Relocation / Location / Commute 10. Need / Want to Make More Money 11. Unstable Organization or Finances / Fear of Layoff

What is immediately obvious from this way of looking at the eleven reasons why people leave is that most of them fall into categories where Hiring Managers can exert a significant amount of influence and control. Only in the case of # IV., Environmental Factors, can it be stated with any degree of certainty that Hiring Managers don't have much to say about an employee's decision to leave. If the employee needs to relocate to another part of the country for family reasons, for example, or if his or her financial needs change dramatically, or if the company's financial situation is so dire that his or her job is threatened, there may not be much the Hiring Manager can do beyond offering counseling and reassurance.

The other three categories – # I., Management Factors, # II., Performance Factors, and # III., Motivational Factors – ARE areas where Hiring Managers can make a critical difference. They are also areas where highly successful companies tend to shine. The critical specifics that appear under these three headings are important enough that we'll be devoting an entire Chapter to them -- Chapter 7: *Keeping the Keepers*. For now, here are six key questions to ask yourself that are based on the list of reasons for employee turnover that will help you prepare your thoughts:

Key Questions about Turnover

If there's conflict with the Manager, is it:

- A disagreement about policy?
- A misunderstanding or miscommunication?
- A performance issue?
- A personality mismatch?

Key Questions about Turnover

Does the Manager:

- Tolerate differing work styles and lifestyles?
- Support Employees with training and tools?
- Foster Employee focus and concentration?
- Make him/herself accessible one-on-one?
- Communicate frequently with staff?
- Update staff on the important issues?

Does each Employee:

- Get regular feedback on how he/she is doing?
- Know what's expected daily/weekly/monthly?

Has the Manager:

- Instituted a performance recognition program?
- Laid out each Employee's development plan?

Is the Manager:

- Sensitive to different Employee personalities?
- Fair in his/her dealings with all staff?
- Flexible on rules without sacrificing fundamentals?

Hiring Right Sets the Foundation

The process that allows you to hire right, as outlined in Chapter 2 – *We Hire for Skills, Fire for Personality* -- can contribute a great deal to the goal of reducing employee turnover as well. It adds value in three ways:

1. **By focusing on the candidates' Soft Skills as well as Hard Skills, it helps you make more reliable candidate selections. The candidates you select will be much more likely to make it through the initial transition to your department or team, and will be less likely to leave, either voluntarily or because of performance issues.**

2. **By probing Behavior, Attitude and Work Ethic (BAW), and Attitude, Interest and Motivation (AIM), you will learn a great deal more about the people you hire. This will set a strong foundation for working with your employees over the long haul.**

3. **You will also pick up insights about your employees' personalities that will allow you to understand their unique styles and to communicate with them more effectively. This "personality sense" will allow you to avoid misunderstandings, match them with appropriate assignments, help them develop satisfying career paths and get more accurate readings on their ongoing needs and moods.**

These three contributions are important because once good employees have been hired, the central issue in preventing employee turnover is establishing and maintaining a healthy pattern of Manager-Employee communication: its frequency, its quality and its content. Take another look at the Key Questions About Turnover in the table above and you'll see that most of them orbit around Manager-Employee communication.

Expanding the Motivational Envelope

As organizational structures have continued to flatten, one casualty has been the myth of the upwardly mobile career path. With so few layers of management remaining in most organizations, fewer people than ever before believe in their chances for climbing to the higher levels. As achieving top management status has come to be seen as an improbable goal, personal lifestyle and work-life balance aspirations have come to take their places alongside "climbing the career ladder" as central vocational themes.

While this is a healthy trend and a realistic adjustment to the forces at work in the marketplace, it is sometimes difficult for Hiring Managers to know what motivates the new style of worker. Certainly, the old "ladder games" -- i.e., "do this and I'll reward you by promoting you to that" – don't work as well with these workers. Instead, these new-style employees are much more interested in the following:

1. **The nature of the task, its importance, and how it fits in with the corporate mission;**

2. **The team – its members and their strengths -- how decisions will be made within the group – their work style;**

3. **What new approaches, techniques and technologies can be learned by doing the job; and,**

4. **The rewards – monetary and otherwise, immediate and mid-term.**

This new emphasis on task, team and work process sometimes leads Hiring Managers to the conclusion that this new breed of employee is "not highly motivated," or is so driven by personal comfort that long-term goals requiring short-term sacrifices can no longer be sustained.

As a consequence, these Hiring Managers evaluate this new type of employee on a project basis only, never considering him or her as a long-term contributor to the company.

This is a mistake. It does a disservice to the talents of the workers being considered and undermines the company's prospects for growth. For what has happened is really very simple. Having abandoned the idea that there will be room for them at the top of the corporation, these workers have begun to focus on the work itself, seeking satisfaction more from the experience of doing the job than from the promise of a long-term reward. As a result, these new workers tend to enjoy their jobs more, and to work together better in teams, than their predecessors ever did.

Most of the roles these new workers perform are as knowledge workers, adding value to a company's products or services through the specialized knowledge they develop on the job or bring to it. With significant vertical growth a virtual impossibility, the day-to-day equity a knowledge worker seeks is horizontal expansion – personal growth into new tasks and technologies, new learning, fresh challenges, projects, tools, teams and goals. While theirs is a less hierarchical approach to career development than that of their predecessors, these new kinds of employees with the new styles of work hold at least as much value for the agile, technologically-driven businesses of the current age as the "corporate ladder" types have for the older-style corporate monoliths.

Here's the punch line. The next time a candidate asks you about the team, the task, the mission and the work processes, don't dismiss him or her as "unmotivated," or unfit for the corporate culture, or a short-term player. Dig deeper instead, understanding that there is more room for horizontal growth in your company than the vertical model could ever provide. And when you dig deeply enough to discover a towering talent, make every effort to hire and retain him or her on his or her own terms, secure in the knowledge that it takes many different types of people, personalities and motivations to make your company thrive and grow.

Characteristics of a Top Hire

If building a team of capable, cooperative, excited and stable employees is part of your strategy for adding value to your company or department – as it should be – then you will need to be looking at the candidates you interview from more than just the perspective of whether their Hard Skills match the task and how they will fare on the first projects that are assigned to them.

Hiring from a perspective that encompasses both Hard Skills and personality factors is no longer just a sound management practice. It has become a business reality and a competitive necessary as well. As the U.S. economy continues its transition from manufacturing to service – with 65% of all jobs now "service" related and just 35% remaining in the "production" sector – it is the character of a company's employees that defines its competitive edge. Even in the manufacturing sector, where the U.S. is challenged to compete with firms with much lower labor costs overseas, it is most often the company's "service" posture that adds the final elements that make the difference between growth and extinction.

Whether you are currently in manufacturing or service, here are four characteristics of the core employees you'll be looking for that cut across all levels, disciplines, occupations and specialties and will ALWAYS be important components of the success profiles you seek:

Characteristics of a Top Hire

Energy	• Does this candidate have a high energy level? • Does he/she have the stamina for long projects? • Is he/she capable of intense, concentrated work? • Will he/she stay with an assignment in the face of unforeseen difficulties? • Can (and will) he/she see tasks through to their completion?
Flexibility	• Can this candidate do multiple tasks and wear more than one hat? • Is he or she still growing, eager to learn, able to take direction and willing to change? • Can he/she work well both in teams and alone? • Will he/she make needed adjustments without losing sight of basic principles or objectives?

(continued)

Characteristics of a Top Hire

Intelli-gence	• Is this candidate quick to grasp new concepts and make logical leaps? • Can he/she anticipate long-term consequences of short-term actions? • Can he/she make decisions when faced with conflicting or confusing information? • Does he/she possess common sense and street smarts? • Is he/she intellectually curious?
Integrity	• Does this candidate honor past agreements? • Does he/she seek the truth and to be truthful? • Is he/she reliable, both in what he/she does and in the validity of his/her judgments? • Does he/she "fess up" in the face of mistakes? • Is he/she accountable and does he/she take responsibility for his/her own actions?

How do these characteristics help reduce turnover?

Four ways:

1. **This kind of employee will always be of value to you and your organization, and therefore will be someone you'll make a concerted effort to keep.**

2. **Because of the integrity factor, this person is the least likely to be the type of employee who will "surprise" you with a resignation one day. Instead, he or she will have the "gumption" to attempt to work out any issues with you up front.**

3. **Because of his or her flexibility, this employee will find ways to adjust to changing circumstances, continuing to find value in the work environment you provide.**

4. **He or she will set a positive example for others, contributing to a supportive work environment and helping bond the team.**

Remember what we said in Chapter 2 – *We Hire for Skills, Fire for Personality* -- about Hard Skills versus Soft Skills? The table of characteristics shown above is a prime example of the need for including a healthy dose of Soft Skills in your assessment. Virtually all of the items shown in this Characteristics list are Soft Skills, elements of character and personality rather than training and experience.

This is not to say that reducing turnover is only about the character of the people you hire. Hiring right sets the foundation, and it is a truism that if you hire poorly, there will be almost nothing you can do keep your company or department's turnover in line. But the solutions to the rest of the retention challenge will still come from what you do on a day-by-day basis in your role as Manager.

Using Exit Interviews as Proactive Tools

Once you've put the proper hiring process in place, your next step in reducing turnover is to get a solid handle on what internal problems need to be solved. The best way to do this is to make exit interviews a standard part of your process whenever someone leaves the company. In order to make those exit interviews effective, make sure you have a structured interview format in place and a standard form for recording the employee's responses. You'll also need to be sensitive to the difficult and confidential nature of the exit interview process from the point of the view if the exiting employee – for example, if you are the person to whom the exiting employee reported, then you may be the LAST person to whom that employee may feel comfortable telling the unvarnished truth. It is also important to understand and honor the fact that exit interviews are voluntary. If the employee states that he/she does not want to participate, and if you have then explained the confidentiality of the process and stressed its value, it is best not to push it if the employee continues to object.

The following six pointers are designed to help you construct an effective exit interview process:

(facing page)

Exit Interview Pointers

 ### 1. Set a Relaxed and Positive Tone

❖ Select the best person to handle this interview (don't assume it's you).

❖ Reassure the exiting employee about the confidentiality of the session.

❖ Say, "Our purpose here is to find ways to make our company a better place to work. While we will listen very carefully to your input, nothing you say here will attributed directly to you. Please feel free to tell me what you really think."

 ### 2. Allow For Some Warm-Up, Asking Easy Questions First

❖ Begin by confirming some basic facts about the exiting employee's history:

- You started work with the company on _____, correct?
- . . . And you started with the ___ Department on _____, right?
- What were your basic job duties when you started?
- Have they changed? How?

❖ Then segue to some "how long" and "why" questions, i.e.:

- How long have you been thinking of leaving?
- What started you thinking that way?
- Could you develop that a little more?

Exit Interview Pointers

3. Be Receptive -- Your Mission Is to Gather Information For Future Use, Not Defend Policies Or Individuals

❖ Use "third-party" phrases to avoid confrontational answers, i.e.:

- "What could management do to improve ..." rather than "What could John Smith do to improve his management style ..." or, "How badly did John Smith ...".

❖ If a statement challenges you or throws you off guard, buy some time before responding. Say:

- "I appreciate your honesty, _____. Tell me a little more about what you mean."

❖ Stay calm. If the exiting employee starts to get too emotional or confrontational, say:

- "_____, you obviously feel very strongly about this, but I'd like to ask you to calm down a bit and suggest some specific actions we could take to improve that in the future."

(continued)

Exit Interview Pointers

 ### 4. Make Sure Your Questions Cover the Bases

◈ Your questions will want to cover the following topics:

- Where is the exiting employee going?
- How will his/her new job duties differ?
- Why did he/she decide to leave?
- How does he/she feel about:
  - ◆ Supervisor and coworkers
  - ◆ Training
  - ◆ Clarity of job duties and goals
  - ◆ Career growth options / career path
  - ◆ Recognition for achievements
  - ◆ Compensation, bonuses, benefits
  - ◆ Management philosophy or style
  - ◆ Policies on hours, dress
  - ◆ Territory assignments
  - ◆ Interdepartmental cooperation
  - ◆ General work environment, including health and safety issues
  - ◆ How company utilized his/her skills and talents
  - ◆ Specific changes needed
  - ◆ Ability to address concerns within the department

(continued)

Exit Interview Pointers

5. Be Flexible When the Conversation Flows in a Useful Direction

❖ If the exiting employee opens up to you and needs to spend some time talking about a subject that is relevant but not next on your list, go with it for a while. The list is there to help you redirect the interview when the time is right.

❖ To move on to another topic, do so by saying:

- "_____, you've made some important points, here, and I've made careful note of them. Right now, though, I need to cover some other topics with you. Tell me, ..."

6. Summarize the Exit Interview And Leave it on a Positive Note

❖ Say something like:

- "_____, those are all the questions I have for now. After I've had a chance to go over my notes, I might want to ask one or two follow up questions. I know that these kinds of conversations can be awkward and I want to thank you for speaking with me. We addressed a lot of questions. If there's something I can do for you, or if something else comes to mind that you think I should hear, please contact me confidentially at _____."

Using the Exit Interview Results

If the exit interviews are conducted and recorded in a systematic fashion, you'll begin to discern patterns very quickly. If your company is like most, the responses you'll gather are very likely to fall into the following five general categories:

❑ **Career Opportunities, including:**
- ➢ Perceived opportunity for advancement
- ➢ Presence and/or clarity of career development plan

❑ **Enjoyment of the work, including:**
- ➢ How well the work utilizes the employee's (Hard) skills
- ➢ The employee's "fit" with the job: i.e., the Soft Skill match

❑ **Corporate Leadership, including:**
- ➢ Clarity and strength of vision and mission
- ➢ Management style
- ➢ Overall perception of leadership by employees
- ➢ Level of respect and support received by employees
- ➢ Frequency and level of communication with employees

❑ **Availability of Training and Skills Enhancement, including:**
- ➢ Opportunity to learn new skills/develop new talents
- ➢ Corporate commitment to training and development
- ➢ Chance to keep up with the latest technology

❑ **Compensation/rewards, including:**
- ➢ Base/variable pay
- ➢ Benefits
- ➢ Recognition of contributions
- ➢ Communication regarding performance

These categories are your roadmap, a checklist of potential areas where you can attack specific problems and reduce unwanted turnover in your company or department. When you combine the actions encompassed by this checklist with an effective hiring process, you'll be putting a comprehensive approach to hiring and retaining staff into place designed to punch some mighty craters into those mountains of turnover.

Turnover Prevention

What can you do in your company or department to keep unwanted turnover from becoming a problem in the first place? Here's a list of ten tips that focus on the day-to-day actions you can take as Hiring Manager to attract and retain employees:

(facing page)

Tips to Attract and Retain Employees

1	Pay employees fairly and within a competitive range.
2	Treat each and every employee with courtesy and respect. Show your employees that you care about them as persons, not just as workers.
3	Praise accomplishments and extra effort: • Both large and small • Verbally and in writing – small notes or quick emails will do. • Do it at least 4 more times than you criticize. • Do it promptly (as soon as the accomplishment is observed). • Do it publicly . . . and in private . . . and at regular meetings. • Do it sincerely.
4	Clearly communicate goals, responsibilities and expectations. Keep people informed. No one likes surprises!
5	Recognize performance appropriately and consistently: • Reward outstanding performance (e.g., with promotions and opportunities) • Small thank you gifts . . . gift certificates, movie tickets, etc., go a long way. • Note: do not tolerate sustained poor performance – coach & train or *de-hire*!

Tips to Attract and Retain Employees

6	Involve employees in plans and decisions, especially those that affect them. Solicit their ideas and opinions. Get buy-in. . . . Encourage initiative.
7	Foster Personal Development & Training Programs – Create opportunities for employees to learn and grow. Bring in outside speakers.
8	Employee Referral Bonus – use your employees' own networks to bring in new staff. Create synergy, fit and a "family" atmosphere (caution: not the same as hiring family members, which is not recommended).
9	Recognition Programs – Send birthday and work anniversary greeting cards to employees at home. Hand address and use a personal stamp.
10	Conduct exit interviews using a structured process and a standard form for asking the questions and recording the results. Understand the reasons why people are leaving! Don't shoot the messenger!!

Your Mandate as Manager

Is there anything that you as Hiring Manager can do to develop your department and build company resources that is more important than hiring great employees and giving them good reasons to stay? Probably not. As was illustrated in the beginning of this chapter, voluntary turnover is a HUGE problem in the US, one that operates at a cost that dwarfs defense spending and is about equal to our national expenditure for Health Care. Unwanted turnover is a colossal waste of time, energy and resources which, because so many of its costs and liabilities are variable, insidious and indirect, lies lurking like an iceberg in the unforgiving waters of the corporate struggle for survival.

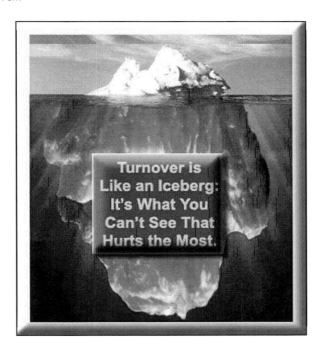

So the task we have before us is really twofold:

1. **To design a hiring process that allows us to hire the people we'll want to keep; and,**

2. **To create a management process that delivers us from the Treadmill of Turnover.**

As we'll see in the ensuing chapters, these two tasks are interrelated and mutually-reinforcing.

Chapter Take-Aways

Item	Idea, Issue or Action Item	Done / Noted
1	Check out our company's turnover statistics for the past two years, comparing them to the national averages.	☐
2	Distribute the turnover cost numbers to key managers. Include the national cost ($2 Trillion per year) and the local cost (3 X Salary per key employee lost).	☐
3	Conduct a brainstorming session with managers on reducing turnover. Make turnover reduction a part of the company's business planning process.	☐
4		☐
5		☐
6		☐
7		☐

Note: The purpose of this "Take-Away" page is to encourage you to summarize the key points of the materials you've read in this Chapter. To get the process started, I have listed three items that I feel are important, but this list is not exhaustive.

Take this opportunity to inventory what you've learned and crystallize what you want to implement before moving on.

Chapter Four

Hiring Blunders
We All
Have Made

As we continue our work to create an optimum hiring process, it would be helpful to illuminate what not to do by reviewing some of the hiring blunders that have been made in the past. We're not talking here about the minor errors that we all commit on occasion, but rather the biggies, those blunders that can put a lethal dent in our objectives. In all, we'll explore 10.5 major errors -- some that are subtle, others that are blatant -- each of which should be avoided like a bathtub full of spiders.

10.5 Major Hiring Blunders

1	Lowering Our Hiring Standards Because We're Under Pressure
2	Making an Offer to a Candidate After the First Interview
3	Making Hiring Decisions Too Much by Gut and Not Enough by Systems and Metrics
4	Qualifying on "Can Do's" to the Exclusion of "Will Do's"
5	Giving Up Too Easily on Reference Checks
6	Blowing the Interview through Lack of Preparation
7	Ignoring the Fact that Time Kills all Deals
8	Hiring People According to the Law of 10's Rather than for their Strengths
9	Talking too Much and Listening Too Little During Interviews
10	Getting Surprised at Offer Time
10.5	Failing to Keep Your Hiring Pipeline Full

Here we go:

Hiring Blunder # 1:

Lowering Our Hiring Standards Because We're Under Pressure

Sometimes in the pressure of hiring under a deadline, we make short-term decisions for the sake of expediency that have negative longer-term consequences. These consequences generally take two forms:

1. **We select the wrong person for the job; or,**
2. **Our negotiation creates an untenable working relationship.**

Here are some examples of how we tend to cave in under pressure:

❖ **We hire someone with insufficient Hard Skills to perform the task the way we need to have it done.**

❖ **We hire someone whose Soft Skills are inappropriate for the role we plan to assign to him or her.**

❖ **We skip critical parts of the hiring process, like assessments, difficult-to-obtain reference checks, technical interviews or introductions to the team.**

❖ **We topple in our negotiations, agreeing to demands that are unreasonable, making adjustments to normal time and attendance requirements, waiving training and indoctrination requirements, or agreeing to compensation that is out of line.**

When we allow any of these things to happen, we give in to a working relationship that is different from what we really want and need. By doing so, we not only betray the agreements we've made with the rest of the team, but we put ourselves in a position where it will be very difficult to manage this person from a position of strength. Having set the wrong tone at the beginning of the relationship, we will soon be challenged to turn the situation around. And the stakes will be high – we'll either have to renegotiate or renege on some of what we've promised the new employee, or we'll be faced with the prospect of lowering our standards for the team as a whole.

These are lousy choices. Rather than put one ounce of effort into trying to fix these situations after they've developed, it's much better to invest all of your energy into making sure they never develop in the first place. Here's a four-point primer on how to do that:

	Hiring From Strength
1	If you are facing a deadline, find a way to compress the amount of time it takes to get the critical hiring steps done rather than skipping some of those steps.
2	Make a list of all your requirements and expectations for the position(s) you want to fill. Then split the list into two columns: negotiables and non-negotiables. Use this list as your compass.
3	Use "preemptory strikes" to keep unreasonable negotiations to a minimum. By making it clear in the early stages that certain things are expected without exception, you'll strengthen your position for later on.
4	Stick to your guns. Once you've stated your "final answer," wait the candidate out. Many times, he or she is testing you. You'll gain more of what you want, and the respect you deserve, in the process.

Vince Lombardi once said that "Fatigue makes cowards of us all." When the pressure is on is exactly the time to dig deeper and summon the personal fortitude to hire from a position of strength, thus avoiding a major hiring blunder.

Hiring Blunder # 2:

Making an Offer to a Candidate
After the First Interview

We've all been through it – a hectic day of interviewing, with no real matches, when suddenly Mr. or Ms. Perfect walks through the door. Everything about this candidate is right, from the credentials on his or her resume, to the image he or she projects and the way he or she conducts him or herself, to his or her carefully crafted answers to your toughest questions and the well-thought-out questions he or she asks in return. The crowning touch is that he or she:

➢ **Has worked on a project that is similar to the one posed by your first job assignment; or,**

➢ **Went to the same school as another successful member of your team; or,**

➢ **Has a background and interests that are very similar to your own – i.e., he or she is the kind of person you'd like to mentor – and perhaps this person even looks and sounds a bit like you.**

Your natural reaction in such a situation is to lunge to capture this perfect candidate before he or she can get away. So you make an offer, either right on the spot, which is a disastrous hiring strategy, or soon after the first interview, which is almost as bad.

Aside from the weak and negative image it conveys about your situation and your company's hiring process, there are three major reasons why making an offer to a candidate during or after the first interview is NOT the way to go:

3 Reasons Not to Jump Too Quickly

1	➢ The candidate does not yet know enough to make an informed decision. If he or she gives you a "yes" now, there's a high probability it will be reversed later.
2	➢ The candidate may not be emotionally ready to accept an offer. ➢ Given that feeling, the candidate's answer is most likely to be "no."
3	➢ Most important, YOU do not yet know enough to make an informed decision. ➢ It's only by meeting a person two or three times over the period of a week or two that you can develop a pattern of impressions that will give you an insight into the candidate's true character, motivations and Soft Skills. ➢ If you lunge after the first interview, you will be making your decision based on "surface" behavior that could very easily be the result of great coaching rather than what the candidate really brings (or doesn't bring) to the table.

The bottom line is this. When you feel tempted to make an offer during or after the first interview, invite the candidate back for a second interview, instead. Give yourself the time to get the input you need to make sure your hiring decision is a valid one before making the offer. Jumping too soon is a blunder you cannot afford.

Hiring Blunder # 3:

Making Hiring Decisions Too Much by Gut And Not Enough by Systems and Metrics

If you are interviewing multiple candidates for a single position, or even if you are going through multiple interviews with a single candidate, it's a mistake to rely on your memory and your intuition to create a pattern by which you'll make the final decision. Here's why:

◈ **You may focus on one aspect of a candidate's background, personality or interviewing behavior – which you either like or dislike -- too much to make an objective decision.**

◈ **If you are meeting with multiple candidates, you may find it difficult to keep their skills and weaknesses straight.**

◈ **Without some external guideposts, you or your team members are likely to miss important hiring steps. These omissions can result in incomplete information or unenthusiastic candidates.**

◈ **As was discussed in some detail in Chapters Two and Three, the interview process alone may not uncover the most important candidate Soft Skills.**

❖ **When making your final selection decision, because your records and notes are incomplete, you may tend to be influenced by your most recent candidate conversations at the expense of information that was generated earlier.**

You don't have to be a statistician to avoid this hiring mistake, nor is it required that all of the tools you use be based on "objective" criteria. Here are three very good reasons to add systems and metrics to your hiring process:

	Why Add Systems & Metrics?	
1	They will enhance your memory as you interview different candidates and help you develop more accurate impressions and comparisons.
2	They will help ensure that the key questions and issues are asked, answered and covered consistently for each candidate.
3	They will provide a format for consolidating your findings as you get down to your final decision.

Adding systems and metrics to your hiring process is an important way to avoid a major hiring blunder, and will be addressed further in the next two chapters.

Hiring Blunder # 4:

Qualifying on "Can Do's" (Hard Skills) To the Exclusion of "Will Do's" (Soft Skills)

In most interviewing and hiring processes involving candidates with prior industry experience, more than 80% of the time is spent on qualifying their Hard Skills, and less than 20% of the time is spent on their Soft Skills. While this tendency to skew the hiring process in the direction of Hard Skills is a natural result of our desire to make sure that the candidates we hire have facility with the systems, procedures, processes, software, products and customers with which we'll be asking them to perform, it is still one of the biggest hiring blunders we can make.

Granted, it's very important in any industry, profession or field of specialization to make sure that the candidate we hire has the basic skills, experience and background needed to do the tasks we're considering assigning to him or her. But as we established in Chapter Two, a candidate's abilities or Can-Do factors alone are not enough. If we want to select someone who can productively transition into our team during his or her first six months and then go on to make a long-term contribution, we'll need to know about his or her Soft Skills -- or Will-Do factors -- as well. For while Can-Do factors are a reasonable gauge of potential, it is the Will-Do factors which are the indicators of success. Can-Do measures aptitude, while Will-Do measures attitude.

Here's a classic example of the difference between Can-Do and Will-Do factors, taken from arena of Sales and Marketing. Let's say that you are interviewing a candidate whose background and experience clearly show strong (hard) skills in prospecting for new customers and opening new territories. That's what the candidate has done in the past. In addition, this candidate has strongly intimated an ability to bring a portfolio of established customers to the table.

Because you are introducing a new product, you need someone who can both prospect and deliver on existing relationships, and this is clearly a candidate who can do both.

But WILL the candidate ACTUALLY DO both? That depends, and is not determined only by what the candidate has done before. If the candidate in our example is tired of climbing the prospecting hill, and would really rather focus on account maintenance and growth, then it is extremely likely that to hire him or her would be a mistake.

The use of Can-Do's alone to qualify and select candidates is based on what seems be a very logical assumption: that past performance predicts future success. But think about this idea for a second. Can-Do's are about Ability; Will-Do's are about Motivation. Or, Can-Do's are about Aptitude, and Will-Do's are about Attitude. Ability and Motivation are two entirely different things, as are Aptitude and Attitude. When the candidate you select has a combination of Can-Do's and Will-Do's that mesh with your objectives for the job, then – and only then – will you have reasonable assurance of a successful hire.

When you are exploring a candidate's Will-Do factors, you will need to employ a different type of questioning and probing. When you're looking for Will-Do, you're not looking so much for what happened in the past as for what's going on inside the candidate right now. And since the questions that get at Will-Do's probe attitudes, personality, motivation and character rather than skills, accomplishments and experience, they tend to be more personal in nature, less predictable in the form they will take, and also more susceptible to fabricated answers.

Because they are more susceptible to fabricated answers, well-crafted Will-Do questions tend to be less direct. To get a handle on why, consider this example: If you were looking for the qualities of honesty, strong work ethic and a high degree of professionalism (or commitment to professional advancement), the LAST thing you would want to do is to ask a candidate the following direct questions:

1. **How honest are you?**
2. **Do you consider yourself a hard worker?**
3. **Do you value your profession?**

Why not? Because the questions you are asking *telegraph* to the candidate what answers you want to hear. Given those kinds of prompts, it's a rare candidate indeed who would answer in any other way but the following:

1. **Very honest;**
2. **Yes – I work very hard;**
3. **My profession is very important to me.**

While it could be argued that a skilled interviewer could make something meaningful out of those answers through a series of follow-up questions, they would still be dealing with a candidate who is now in the position of "defending" his or her original responses, rather than one who is expressing how he or she really thinks or feels.

Because the "Will-Do" questions are a little more challenging to think up and remember, it is highly recommended that you have a list of them written out before you begin your interviewing process. This way, you're less likely to forget to ask them in the press of the moment and more likely to ask them in the proper manner. To help you with the task of developing your list of "Will-Do," questions, here's a list of five to get you started:

Probing the "Will-Do's"

1	You have an interesting background. If you had the freedom to design your own most logical next career step, what would it be? ... Could you expand on that? ... Is that important to you? ... Why?
2	What are your five top work activities on a daily basis? ... (Make notes.) Which of those five are "want to do's" and which are "have to do's"? ... Why?
3	Give me an example of a time when you had to bend the rules or go outside the lines to get something done. ... How did you do it? ... How often have situations like that occurred in the past?
4	I think you've had a chance to review the job description and talk about the requirements of the job, am I right? Knowing yourself as you do, how would you advise your next supervisor to manage you?
5	Tell me about a time when a project you were working on, either alone or as part of a team, got seriously behind schedule. How did that make you feel and what did you do about it? ... And the results? ...

You'll note that the "Will-Do" questions are each actually a question and a series of follow-ups, and that they deal with situations, choices and values as well as facts. Your purpose in asking them is to get at the candidate's Soft

Skills – i.e., the candidate's motivations, attitudes, character and personality traits without "telegraphing" what answers you want to hear. These questions are successful when they generate a conversation that gives you insights – either positive or negative – into how the candidate thinks, or "ticks," and thus how he or she will approach the real-life aspects of the job you are trying to fill.

By implementing "Will-Do" probes like these as a part of your hiring process, you'll avoid a major hiring blunder and achieve a healthier balance between Ability and Motivation, Aptitude and Attitude.

Hiring Blunder # 5:

Giving Up Too Easily On Reference Checks

We live in a litigious society, and because we do, meaningful reference verifications are becoming more difficult to obtain. Yet references are among the most important tools at our disposal, as they represent the experiences, opinions and recommendations of the people to whom our candidates have reported in the past. When we decide to hire people without the benefit of meaningful references, we commit a major hiring blunder.

In order to compensate for a lack of meaningful reference information, some Hiring Managers have resorted to using multiple sources for obtaining "public domain" information on the candidate, i.e., credit checks, criminal background checks, academic credential checks and the like, and combining them with the cursory information that is available through pro-forma reference information from Human Resources. There is no question that this approach will give you some useful information, but consider the type:

1. **The typical criminal background check will tell you whether a candidate has been convicted of (but not arrested for) a crime in a certain county within a certain period of time.**

2. **The typical credit check will tell you about the candidate's average bill payment record, and whether or not he or she has declared bankruptcy in the recent past.**

3. **The typical academic credentials check will confirm the candidate's degrees, and in some cases will provide his or her transcripts or overall grade point average.**

4. **The typical cursory reference check with Human Resources will confirm work dates, ballpark compensation, and (sometimes) eligibility for re-hire. In other words, name, rank and serial number, only.**

While this information all has its place, it sets a very low baseline. It tells you that your candidate is not a bank robber, not a deadbeat, not a fraud or not an employee who went postal the last time he or she changed jobs. What it doesn't tell you is how this candidate compares with others in the same field, or whether a former employer thinks that he or she would be a good fit for the specific assignment you have in mind, or how best to manage him or her. And because *none* of those third-party sources *are* the person whose team or department depended on the candidate to help them meet their goals, their responses will not have the same authority as those you'd hear by speaking with a direct supervisor.

Here are six tips for getting the references you need:

Getting Meaningful References

1	Before asking a candidate for a list of references, stress that you want to speak with his or her former supervisors. Review the list with the candidate to verify that that's what you've received.
2	Make sure you use a reference form that probes for job performance, candidate strengths and weaknesses, citizenship, job-related personality traits, and recommendations re: the new job -- as well as for the basics.
3	If you don't have the time to do it yourself, assign the referencing task to someone who has the phone tenacity to get through and the presence to hold his or her own with Managers or Executives like you.
4	If you get stonewalled by one person when verifying a reference with a company, call someone else there and ask for help.
5	When you've completed the first reference on a candidate -- whether it's positive or negative -- do another. Go on to get a second opinion, and a third, if necessary, until you've establish a clear pattern.
6	If all else fails, pose the following question to your candidate: "If I were to talk with _ref's name_ at _____ Company and to ask him or her to give me three adjectives that best describe your job performance there, what would those adjectives be?" ... (Listen and watch very carefully.) ... Then follow up with, "Why those particular words?"

Gathering useful reference information is critical to your ability to make good hiring decisions. Use the steps noted above to help you succeed in your efforts to do so.

Hiring Blunder # 6:

Blowing the Interview
Through Lack of Preparation

For many Hiring Managers, the stark reality is that the steps just before a candidate interview go something like this:

STEP 1: **Fumble around on top of desk (or conduct frantic search online) to find a copy of the candidate's resume.**

STEP 2: **Rampage through supply closet to find a manila folder to put it in.**

STEP 3: **Rummage through wallet or purse to find a business card.**

STEP 4: **Put on jacket, check hair or makeup, straighten tie or accessories.**

STEP 5: **Scan candidate's resume as he or she is being ushered into the office or interviewing room.**

Given these steps, are we actually surprised that so many interviews don't go very well?

Like any other effective meeting, an interview requires preparation. If you value your time, and if you want to maximize your opportunity to gather the information and impressions you need to make a good hiring decision, you'll need to take a few minutes before the interview to gather your thoughts and focus on your objectives.

If you don't prepare, you'll be forced to "wing it," and the following is likely to result:

1. **If you make the candidate wait while you read the resume in front of him or her, you'll convey a negative impression.**

2. **You'll be likely to miss asking a key question that is important to your decision.**

3. **If you seem hurried, distracted or disorganized, the candidate may conclude that the hire isn't very important to you.**

4. **Without a clear objective, the interview may wander off course, focusing on topics that squander time and are irrelevant to the hire.**

This is not to say that you are going to need a detailed outline in order to conduct what is intended to be an open and free-flowing conversation. But you will need a basic agenda, and a few notes about how you want that conversation to proceed. Here are some pointers:

Preparation Pointers

	Review the requirements and objectives of the job you want to fill. Bring the key points into focus.
	Review the candidate's resume or data sheet. Jot down the questions it brings to mind and highlight the items you'd like to explore in depth.

Preparation Pointers

	Develop a list of bullet points of the topics you want to cover during the interview. Keep it handy as a navigation device.
	Have a pad or sheet of paper ready for taking notes. Write down the candidate's name, along with the date and time of the interview, at the top of the sheet. (Avoid putting interview impressions in the margins of the resume, as this information may well end up in the Candidate's personnel file.)
	If you are interviewing several candidates in a row, plan about 30 minutes of "cushion time" between each interview. This way you'll be able to consolidate your impressions of the first candidate before preparing for and speaking with the second.

Interviewing is an instance where a little preparation will enable you to cover a lot of ground. By investing the ten minutes or so it takes to implement the pointers presented above, you'll conduct more effective and consistent interviews, and avoid this hiring blunder.

Hiring Blunder # 7:

Ignoring the Fact that Time Kills All Deals

One of the worst mistakes you can make as a Hiring Manager is to let your hiring process take too long from the first interview to the offer decision, as time kills all deals. The fact that job change has been identified as one of the top five human stressors only makes the issue of time that much more compelling.

No matter what the unemployment statistics may say at any given time, Hiring Managers live in a competitive jungle when it comes to attracting and hiring the best candidates. For even in the worst economic climate, these candidates find a way to keep working, and will not move unless the new opportunities are obviously better than the ones they would be giving up. So Hiring Managers are competing against two adversaries for the best candidates:

1. **Other potential employers who also want to hire them; and,**

2. **Their own natural tendencies, as their stress levels increase, to hunker down stay where they are.**

Candidates are faced with the same decision-making dilemmas as you are as they go through your hiring process. Just like you, they are required to make their decisions with incomplete information and a cloudy crystal ball. As a result, they tend to make their decisions symbolically, rather than logically, emotionally rather than rationally. They will invariably judge your opportunity as much by the way the hiring process makes them *feel* as by what you and your co-workers say to them.

While there are many things you can do to make your hiring process more competitive, the most pressing one is to take control of the amount of time takes from your first interview with the candidate until the offer is made. For when a hiring process takes too much time to get to the offer step, the best candidates you are interviewing will quickly conclude:

1. That you're really not *that* interested in them; or,

2. That you're not decisive enough to represent the kind of company they want to work for.

Whatever they conclude, these are effective candidates with strong Hard and Soft Skills and notable accomplishments. Even if they have small Ego's, these are busy folks who have other options. The fact that your interview process seems to have initially gone well will reinforce their confidence about their own marketability. This new sense of confidence will radiate back into their own work environments, and perceptive managers with the authority to do something about it will sit up and take notice. Headhunters will call with other opportunities, or some relative or business associate will refer them to another company. Because your lengthy hiring process is conveying the signal that you are no longer that interested in them, these candidates will rapidly lose interest in your opportunity, as well. With the passage of just a little more time, something definitive will happen. Either they will get promoted, take another job, or remove themselves from the market.

The bottom line is this. In order to make your hiring process work in a highly competitive market, you need to make sure that it is effective, expedient and decisive. In general, the amount of time it takes from the first interview to the offer should not exceed the following guidelines:

Hiring Time Frames

Job Level or Type	Time Brackets
Executive	Four - Six Weeks
Manager, Director	Four Weeks
Individual Contributor, 1st Level Supervisor	Two Weeks
Difficult-to-Find Individual Contributors	One Week
Entry-Level, Unless Hard-to-Find	Two – Four Weeks

This is not to say that you should skip important hiring steps in order to achieve these time frames. Rather, your challenge is to compress the amount of time it takes to get those steps completed. When you do so, you'll enhance your performance in this hyper-competitive employment market and avoid a major hiring blunder.

Hiring Blunder # 8:

Hiring People According to the Law of 10's Rather than For their Strengths

Have you ever heard of the Law of 10's? That's the one where each person you hire is ten percent weaker than the one you hired before, until you've built a team around you that is subservient, yielding, and dependent upon your detailed direction for every idea and action. It's not a pretty picture, particularly in this current age of flattened organizational structures, when the best employees wear multiple hats and distinguish themselves by taking on assignments outside the boundaries of their job descriptions.

How does the Law of 10's come to pass? It happens when the hiring selections we make are driven more by personal comfort than by the requirements of the job or the pragmatic objectives of building the team. It often begins after a bad hiring experience when a Hiring Manager brings someone on board with great talent and promise, who then gets out of control or becomes unreliable. In order to avoid repeating this experience, the Hiring Manager reacts by going into a defensive hiring shell. In this mode, the Hiring Manager begins to equate "talent and promise" with "uncontrollability" or "unreliability," and proceeds to hire only those people whom he or she is certain will not "be a problem," whether they have the Hard and Soft Skills to excel at the job or not. As more people of this sort continue to join the team, group performance ratchets downward, eventually threatening to drag your career as a Hiring Manager down with it.

Another variant of the Law of 10's occurs in very large organizations. There the Law makes itself known by moving progressively down through the corporate hierarchy, as each new person who is hired is 10% weaker than the person to whom he or she reports, creating the same downward spiral of talent and performance. This has become such a virulent problem in some corporations that it has prompted top Executives there (as former General Electric CEO Jack Welch relates in his book, *Jack: Straight from the Gut,* Warner Books, 2001) to embark on programs where they replace as many as 10% of their workforce every year just to upgrade their internal talent pool.

Fortunately, there are other methods available for combating the Law of 10's that focus on avoiding such mistakes with new hires and are therefore not quite so draconian. We'll be introducing them in the next chapter.

84

Hiring Blunder # 9:

Talking Too Much and Listening Too Little During Interviews

Have you ever had the experience of interviewing a candidate, walking away with a favorable impression, and then realizing that you didn't get the information you needed to determine whether or not he or she would really perform the job to your standards? While the conversation may have been engaging, this mistake will be costly, as it interferes with your ability to do your job as Hiring Manager.

One thing you want to avoid at all costs when interviewing is to get into a situation where you do all the talking. You DON'T want to be like Mr. Mouthears, below, whose mouth has switched places with his ears, and whose ears have been fused together and zippered shut:

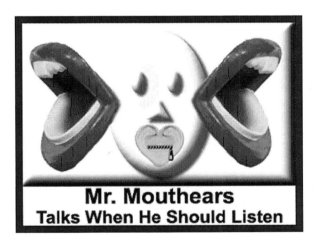

Mr. Mouthears
Talks When He Should Listen

As you probably know from having been one at one time or another, candidates are routinely coached -- in how-to books and by outplacement firms and headhunters -- to come to interviews armed with questions of their own. It's part of *their* strategy to get *you* talking as much as possible.

As the person conducting the interview, it is your prerogative and responsibility to control the conversation. While you do want the interview to be a two-way street, and to respond to the candidate's legitimate need for information, the challenge is to do so in a way that does not interfere with your ability to get the information you need.

To do that, I recommend that you hone your skills on these three techniques for controlling interview conversations:

Interview Control Techniques

1 For Your Questions Of the Candidate

❖ Use open-ended questions – i.e., questions that begin with "Who, What, When, Where, Why, How" -- for probing during the interview.

❖ But be selective about which of those questions you use.

❖ For example, the "Why" and "How" questions will generate much longer answers than the "Who," "What," "Where" and "When" questions, and should be used mainly for exploring values or evaluating technical depth.

(continued)

Interview Control Techniques

2 For Your Responses To the Candidate's Questions

❖ Limit your initial responses to candidate questions to 30 seconds or less, providing a sound byte rather than a narrative.

❖ You can always follow up if the candidate requests more information.

❖ You can also change the direction of the conversation.

3 For Changing Direction And Keeping the Interview On Track

❖ If you are responding to a candidate's question, say, "That's a good question, _____, and the short answer is . . . (sound byte). I'm sure we can develop this further later on, if need be. But for now, I need to focus on something else. Tell me, what (or who, when, where, why or how) ..."

❖ If the candidate is engaged in a monologue, break in and say, "_____," you're making an interesting point, but I need to focus on something *else* right now. Tell me, what (or who, when, where, why or how) ..."

In general, your interviews will be much more productive if you keep them crisp and to the point. If you are the one who is asking most of the questions, then it follows that your candidates will be doing most of the talking. If you use the interview control techniques presented above, you'll be able to control the direction and flow of that talk, and get the information you need to make an informed decision.

Here are some rules of thumb for managing your interviews:

Interviewing Rules of Thumb

 ### Who Should Talk How Much:

❖ You should talk no more than 35% of the time.
❖ The candidate should talk no less than 65% of the time.

 ### Who Should Be Asking Most Of The Questions:

❖ You should ask most of the questions.
❖ When you are tracking well with the candidate, those questions will be free flowing and intuitive.
❖ When things begin to stall a bit, you'll need to go back to "Who, What, When, Where, Why and How."

 ### How Much Time The Interviews Should Take:

❖ Introductory telephone interviews, 10 – 15 minutes max; 20 – 25 minutes for technical candidates.
❖ Introductory face-to-face screening interviews: 30 minutes, max.
❖ Subsequent interviews: 45 minutes; no longer than an hour.
❖ Note: Interviews that last 90 minutes or more are usually counterproductive.

Interviewing Rules of Thumb

 ### How the Interviews Should Be Paced:

❖ In general, any more than 5-7 minutes spent on one topic is too long.

❖ A series of 2-3 shorter interviews is better than one long one (NEVER make an offer during or right after the first interview).

❖ Meet your candidate(s) in a series of 45-minute interviews over a period of a week or two rather than trying to get the entire process done in one longer session.

❖ This "series" approach will give you a better handle by which to gauge the candidate's character and to establish a pattern of behavior.

The flip side of the interviewing coin is that, if you are the one who is asking most of the questions, then you'll also be the one who's doing most of the listening. You will be listening for consistency, for tone and undertone, for nuance, for intensity, conviction, character and commitment. And listening is the most important – and least exercised – skill of all. By developing your questioning and listening skills as a Hiring Manager, you'll accelerate your progress toward three major objectives:

1. **You'll convey skills as a Hiring Manager to the candidate simply by the way you conduct yourself;**

2. **You'll manage your time efficiently and get the most out of each interview; and,**

3. **You'll achieve the insights and information you need as a Hiring Manager to make sounder hiring decisions.**

You'll also avoid a major hiring blunder.

Hiring Blunder # 10:

Getting Surprised at Offer Time

There's nothing like a last-minute surprise at offer time to kill the transaction and ruin your day. Rather than being a time when you're forced to grapple with a fistful of last-minute details, an offer, when handled well, should almost be anticlimactic. This does not mean that the candidate knows ahead of time that he or she has won the job – but that fact should be the only, and final, surprise. Rather, it means that you should have handled all of the other issues up front, prior to making the formal offer. When they're not properly handled before the offer, these issues are like a nest of adders in a gradual-release capsule. They have an uncanny way of rearing their ugly, flat heads and injecting you with their toxins when you least expect them.

Here are two ways you can prevent these vipers from poisoning your hires:

1. **MONEY** -- You and the candidate have different expectations about money. This is a very common problem at offer time that often squashes the hire. Sometimes the cause of this is a set of external forces that are working on the candidate, but as often as not, the source of the problem is a lack of clarity on the money issue on your part prior to the offer being made. It's your responsibility to make sure that the money has been clearly defined and is acceptable to the candidate before you make the offer. You can do that by asking an hypothetical offer question during the second or third

interview, saying something like this: "If we decide to offer you this position, the amount we're prepared to pay would not exceed $_____ (be certain to quote a number on the low side, here). Is that amount acceptable to you?" Make sure your question is crisp and precise, and then listen very carefully to the content, tone and inflection of the candidate's answer. If you settle for anything other than a solid, emphatic "Yes" now, then you're probably in for a sad surprise later.

2. **COUNTEROFFER** -- The candidate accepts your offer, and then succumbs to a counter-offer from his or her current company. As organizational structures continue to get flatter and slimmer, the tendency for companies to make counteroffers to prevent key employees from leaving is on the rise. To deal with this trend, make sure that you know your candidate's leanings on this issue – as well as his or her true motivations for making the move – well prior to making the offer. Then be mentally prepared for the certainty that a counter-offer attempt will happen, and be ready to support the candidate through his or her resignation and its aftermath. Here's a primer:

Countering the Counter Offer	
1	Well before you make an offer, but after you've tested the offer amount with the candidate, ask the candidate to project him/herself into the situation where he/she is meeting with his/her manager to resign.
2	Ask, "What do you think your Manager will say?"
3	Then ask, "How will you to respond to that?"

Countering the Counter Offer

4	If he or she does not bring up counter offer, ask, "Do you think your manager will offer you more money or a promotion or a transfer or more authority or more interesting responsibilities to convince you to stay?"
5	If he or she says "No," say, "Well, let's assume your manager does make you a counter offer. What will you do?
6	Listen very carefully to the candidate's response. If the candidate says he or she won't accept the counter, respond a little skeptically. Say, "Really?" Then ask the candidate, "Why not?"
7	Listen carefully to the candidate's response, and reinforce it if it makes sense. Help the candidate with additional reasons from your own perspective about why accepting a counter offer is a bad move.
8	If the candidate gives you anything other than a definitive and well-supported "No" when you ask the counter offer question, then any offer you make will be at risk. Under those circumstances, you are best advised not to make it at all.

Being ready for a counter-offer in this marketplace may mean using a double-offer strategy, as well. Using this strategy, you would have one offer that you would make, and a "sweetener" that you would keep in your pocket, to be used only if necessary, once a counter-offer is made. If you present the sweetener to the candidate, make sure that you test it as an hypothetical first, just as you did with the offer, and then draw your line in the sand by conveying in no uncertain terms that this adjustment to your original offer is your "last and best."

In a more general sense, surprises happen at offer-time because decisions about career moves are stressful to a majority of candidates, who tend to procrastinate on addressing the emotional realities of the job change until you put their feet to the fire by making them an offer. As a result, issues, details and problems that could have been handled early on have a way of staying submerged until the very end. Even then, many candidates will not be able to articulate their concerns. All a candidate will often be able to say is, "I have a strange feeling in my gut, but I can't put my finger on what it is." In the face of that feeling, when presented with an offer and a deadline, that candidate is very likely to turn the offer down.

Here are some pointers that will help you bring these hidden concerns to the surface:

Surfacing Hidden Concerns

 Ask each candidate to articulate his or her questions and concerns about the job at each step in the interview process. Address them as they're identified, making careful notes.

 Be skeptical when a candidate says he or she doesn't have any concerns. This is a clear sign of emotional procrastination. Ask a series of "What about this?" questions that focus on potential concerns to dig out the issues that are hidden below the surface.

Surfacing Hidden Concerns

 Prior to making the offer, revisit the concerns that were already identified and handled. Ask the candidate if he or she is "still OK," with them, and then challenge him or her to tell you why.

If a candidate confides in you that he or she has a concern that he or she "can't put my finger on" after you make an offer, treat it as an opportunity rather than a pain. Rather than turn the offer down, this candidate is giving you an option to turn him or her around. Thank him or her for giving your offer "such serious consideration." Then use a variant of the pointers shown above. This will give you the chance to identify the problem, fix it, and clear the way for the candidate to say, "Yes!"

Hiring Blunder # 10.5:

Failing to Keep Your Hiring Pipeline Full

For many Hiring Managers, hiring isn't something they do every day. It tends to be an activity that happens just frequently enough to serve as an interruption to the ongoing flow of their work and yet just seldom enough that they always feel a little "rusty" when doing it. It is no wonder, then, that Hiring Managers are often guilty of three lapses that are detrimental to their goals:

1. **They relegate the activities of hiring to the lower rungs of the priority ladder;**

2. **They delegate too many of those hiring activities to people on their staff who don't have the skills, the**

savvy or the authority to conduct them properly; and,

3. **They let their "hiring pipeline" get empty – i.e., they have no prospective candidates lined up and are forced to "start from scratch" the next time an opening occurs.**

It may be understandable when Hiring Managers allow these lapses to occur, but it's also distressing, as the costs can be very high. Here are some of the major downsides:

Hiring Lapses & Downsides

1   <u>**Making Hiring A Low Priority Activity**</u>:

❖ **When hiring is treated as a low priority activity, key steps tend to get skipped and the process becomes too informal and casual to be effective. Candidates sense this as "lack of commitment" and the best ones will lose interest in the opportunity.**

Hiring Lapses & Downsides

2 Delegating Hiring Activities to The Wrong People:

❖ When key hiring activities (for example, screening, interviewing and conducting reference checks) are delegated to people who cannot handle them well, then the best prospective candidates tend to get passed over, and the quality of the information available to make the hiring decision is sketchy and inconclusive.

3 Failing to Keep the Hiring Pipeline Full:

❖ Given national turnover statistics, the Hiring Manager of an "average" company will lose at least 20% of his or her staff every year, and in some industries more than twice that amount. Given these numbers, it only makes sense to always be looking for the next hire. Without being proactive in this way, unnecessary delays, costs and revenue losses will result whenever a new position is created or an employee leaves.

Hiring lapse # 3 deserves special attention, as its remedy can often provide a partial cure for lapses #1 and #2, as well. Simply stated, a Hiring Manager should always be on the lookout for his or her next hire, whether he or she has current openings or not. He or she should know, instinctively, whom the first contact would be to find a replacement for every key person in the department. By doing so, he or she is *building bench strength*, shoring up the firm's ability to respond quickly and effectively to unexpected changes in staffing needs. By staying personally involved in assessing potential hires, and knowing who could be hired for each key position on relatively short notice, the Hiring Manager will remain sharp and be in an excellent position to judge the recruiting and hiring IQ of the internal staff members he or she is using to help complete certain hiring tasks.

One of the best features of the "always searching for the next hire" mode is that it takes the deadline pressure out of the recruiting process, and allows you as Hiring Manager to use informal networking as a primary source of candidate referrals. Here's a partial list of the kinds of network sources you should be tapping regularly to keep your hiring pipeline full:

Sources for Filling Your Pipeline

- ❖ Finalists or semifinalists from prior hiring activities

- ❖ Referrals from your employees. (Referral Bonus Program -- $500 @ 60 days, $500 @ 120 days)

- ❖ Unsolicited resumes that match the skills and characteristics of the department

- ❖ Business associates in similar industries or job functions

- ❖ Customers or customer prospects (who do THEY know who is good?)

- ❖ Internal employees who are ready for a step up

- ❖ Other department heads

Sources for Filling Your Pipeline

◈ **Trade and Professional Association meetings**

◈ **Business networking events**

◈ **Vendors and salespeople who call on you**

◈ **People from any industry who impress you with their Hard and Soft Skills, if only as a source of referrals to others with similar background and character**

Because you are working without a specific deadline when you build bench strength, you can afford to take the time to nurture relationships for the longer term. Just make sure that you are absolutely realistic about what can be expected by the people you're nurturing -- particularly during periods when they are unemployed or actively seeking a job change.

Let them know in no uncertain terms whether or not you currently have a position to fill. Once the air has been cleared on that issue, you will find that most people will be respond positively to an invitation to an exploratory conversation, with the idea in mind that some way of profiting from what is learned there will arise in the future. And who knows, in addition to building your bench strength, you *may* meet someone with such impressive Hard and Soft Skills that you'll feel compelled to create a position for him or her where none existed before.

How much time should you invest in building the bench strength of your organization? That depends on the level of turnover you are experiencing, and on the nature of the job functions you supervise. If you are in a higher turnover industry or function like hospitality or some areas of sales, you should invest a minimum of two hours per week when you have no current openings, and a great deal more than that when you do. And in any case, your investment of time should NEVER go below four hours per month.

For people who are truly skilled at building bench strength, the issue is not as much about time invested as it is about attitude maintained. These top hiring practitioners carry an attitude of alertness whereby they are ALWAYS on the lookout for their next hire.

Being proactive in your recruiting and hiring practices is more critical now than ever before. During the past two decades, major changes have swept the world economy that have forced all companies and organizations to trim down and reduce their layers of management to the point where fewer and fewer people are responsible for more and more of their key functions. Accordingly, each of these people is individually responsible for a broader span of products and services than was the case even five years ago.

The people you hire now are thus more important to your organization than ever before. The roles they play are more strategic to your business. As a Hiring Manager, it is your job to assemble the best possible people for your team, as well as to build your organization's bench strength. How effective a job those people do as individuals, how well they perform as a group, and how quickly you can respond when a key position needs to be filled, can make a HUGE difference to your company, its survival and success.

Hiring well means hiring the right people -- a critically important part of your job. It sets a firm foundation in place for leading and managing your organization.

By making hiring a proactive and high-priority part of your ongoing routine as a Hiring Manager, you elevate it to the stature it deserves, and avoid this final hiring blunder.

Chapter Take-Aways

Item	Idea, Issue or Action Item	Done / Noted
1	Develop a list of minimum standards and expectations for all hires. Include specific job and skill requirements, citizenship issues, training assignments and compensation limits.	☐
2	Use the examples provided to brainstorm a set of 10 standard questions for probing Soft Skills. Make sure that the questions DO NOT telegraph the desired answers.	☐
3	Build the counter offer steps into our process and train key staff on how and when to use them.	☐
4		☐
5		☐
6		☐
7		☐

Note: The purpose of this "Take-Away" page is to encourage you to summarize the key points of the materials you've read in this Chapter. To get the process started, I have listed three items that I feel are important, but this list is not exhaustive.

Take this opportunity to inventory what you've learned and crystallize what you want to implement before moving on.

Chapter Five

Unleashing the Power of Personality

F or a number of chapters now, I have been asserting that there's another dimension that must be mastered if we are to succeed in hiring right most of the time and in retaining the good people we hire.

That dimension is personality, or the "Soft Skills," as we have come to call them. My purpose here is to share with you the basic concepts of personality as they relate to hiring and retaining and to give you some basic tools that will help you interpret the key signals of personality that surround us all, all of the time.

Different is Different

Let's begin by acknowledging that what we're about to discuss is a topic that can be both controversial and a bit touchy. Some people resist the idea that personality traits or styles can be measured, and others feel uncomfortable and in some cases even outraged about how the findings of some personality tests have been used in the past to classify people in ways that limit their potential. Nonetheless, the theory of personality has well-founded theoretical roots, and has been put to practical and positive use in countless organizations of all sizes throughout the world. For the most part, the results have been beneficial for the people doing the hiring, as well as for the people being hired. And yet like all tools, personality measurement is exactly as good as the purposes for which it is employed, and is only as ethical as the people who use it.

I understand and empathize with these concerns, and have discussed them many times with concerned Hiring Managers across North America. To address the issue, I have adopted the following statement as a mantra for the right way to approach the critical issue of applying personality theory to hiring and managing staff:

➢ **Different is different.**

➢ **Different is not right; nor is it wrong . . .**

➢ **Different means not the same, which is not the same as unequal . . .**

➢ **Different simply means different.**

When we incorporate the teaching that "different simply means different" into our core values, then personality and its measurement becomes a tool for liberation rather than constriction. For rather than focusing on what people cannot do, and thus limiting them, we concentrate on what people do best, thus empowering them to succeed.

The DISC Approach to Personality

The approach to personality measurement that we'll be using here is best known as "DISC," or the DISC Personality Survey. Each of the letters in the "DISC" acronym refers to a cluster of behavior patterns that reflect one of four aspects of the normal human personality:

| **D**ominance |
| **I**nfluence |
| **S**teadiness |
| **C**ompliance |

This concept of four basic personality styles was first articulated in 1928 by Dr. William Moulton Marston, a Harvard University PhD and Columbia University Professor in Psychology who went on to develop the original lie detector test. In creating the DISC system, Dr. Marston built on the pioneering work of noted psychologist Karl Jung, but differed from Jung in that Marston suggested that personality could be distilled into four distinct styles of behavior, versus the 12-16 personality types defined by Jung and his students.

Personality theory became a practical reality during World War II, when Isabel Briggs-Myers and her mother, Katherine C. Briggs, developed the "Myers-Briggs" personality instrument to help the military find better ways of matching defense workers with their assignments. While Myers-Briggs used Jung's concepts for their assessment tool, a DISC-based measurement system soon followed, and numerous applications were found throughout government, business and industry as both tools became more refined. Today DISC and Myers-

Briggs are among the most popular and successful assessment tools being used in the marketplace, with millions of users throughout the world.

My preference for DISC is based on two primary factors. First, the four personality styles make intuitive sense – to me, and to most other people as well. And second, because it distills normal human behavior into a manageable number of personality styles, I find it easy to use. For most Hiring Managers, time is their scarcest resource. In that context, an assessment system that can be administered and interpreted easily is much more practical and useful than one that requires more advanced analysis and complex codes.

Here are five additional reasons to choose the DISC assessment system:

5 Reasons to Choose DISC	
1	Its theoretical underpinnings are well established and academically sound.
2	It's a proven, validated instrument that measures performance by comparing potential new hires to benchmarks created by your own best performers.
3	Its results are easy to understand – it uses Dr. Marston's four categories of response rather than the much larger number of personality types required by other tools.

	5 Reasons to Choose DISC
4	Its outcomes are graphically displayed, allowing the Hiring Manager to determine basic personality styles at a glance.
5	The DISC Profile is easy on the people who take it. It involves 28 multiple-choice questions that can be answered very quickly – usually 5-7 minutes per person will do.

The DISC system makes the following four assumptions that relate to hiring and managing staff:

1. That all people share the four, basic personality styles -- Dominance, Influence, Steadiness and Compliance -- in differing degrees;

2. That all four styles are essential to our performance in the workplace;

3. That it is the differences in how those styles are mixed within each of us that determines our particular degree of "chemistry and fit" – and thus, our success potential -- within a job role or team; and,

4. That knowing how to measure and respond to these differences are essential keys for hiring and managing staff.

Like most personality assessment systems, DISC assumes that people act in predictable patterns, and that even while expressing their differences, they operate within definable boundaries. DISC provides a way to "map" those patterns and boundaries in order to predict behavior. It is thus an important key to measuring Soft Skills.

How prevalent are each of the four DISC styles when distributed over the population? Here is what the survey scores show:

Personality Style	% of Population
Dominance	**18%**
Influence	**28%**
Steadiness	**40%**
Compliance	**14%**

It's important to remember when viewing a chart like this one that every person has a mix of all four personality styles, but that one or two are usually more pronounced than the others. Throughout the remainder of this book, when I refer to someone as a "high 'D'" or "high 'S,C'", for example, I am speaking of that person's prevailing style or styles.

DISC Definitions

Here are some definitions of each of the four personality styles:

D.I.S.C. -- Definitions

D	**D = Dominance.** High "D" individuals are drivers, competitive, forceful, inquisitive, direct, decisive, self-starting and assertive. People with "D" personalities often want to be in charge. They focus on power and results. Their communication style is to "tell," and their management style is authoritarian. They are motivated by tasks completed and accomplishments.
I	**I = Influence.** High "I" individuals are prominent, friendly, impulsive, persuasive, communicative and positive. They seek consensus and build alliances, focusing on people rather than things. They communicate by "selling," and their management style is democratic. They are motivated by attention, recognition, social inclusion, trendiness and status.

(continued)

D.I.S.C. -- Definitions

S	**S = <u>Steadiness</u>. High "S" individuals are dependable, deliberate, good listeners, amiable, kind and persistent. They focus on providing service. They communicate by listening, first, and they manage via precedents and procedures. They are motivated by process, frequency of contact, repeatability, reliability and stability.**
C	**C = <u>Compliance</u>. High "C" individuals are diplomatic, careful, accommodating, precise, logical, systematic, accurate and perfectionists. Their focus is on policy, procedures, numbers and quality. They prefer to communicate through writing rather than- conversation, and they manage via facts and knowledge. They are motivated to find out the details of how things actually work.**

Don't be surprised if, now that you've seen DISC defined and described, it all sounds very familiar. You've probably been exposed to it in some form before. Because of Dr. Marston's pioneering work and the success of the DISC Survey itself, the concepts defined above have gained broad acceptance as a normal part of the daily discourse of business, and terms like Dominance, Influence, Steadiness and Compliance -- or their synonyms -- are often used to describe personalities in the business environment.

To get a handle on your own intuitive sense of what DISC means, take a moment complete the following exercise. It's a simple quiz that asks you to match the behaviors described with one of the four DISC personality styles. Since there are eight questions, the exercise should take only a couple of minutes for you to complete:

Test Your DISC Intuitions

Instructions: For each of the questions listed in the numbered paragraphs below, check one item from the right-hand column that most accurately matches the DISC personality style being described.

1 What personality style would a department manager most likely have if he or she asked the staff to begin every meeting by studying a document or spreadsheet?

☐ Dominance   ☐ Steadiness

☐ Influence   ☐ Compliance

2 What personality style would a person most likely have if he or she had a habit of interrupting presentations by asking the presenter to "get to the point"?

☐ Dominance   ☐ Steadiness

☐ Influence   ☐ Compliance

Test Your DISC Intuitions

3 What personality style would a person most likely have if he or she began every answer to a "how to" question by saying, "The way we've done it in the past is ..."?

❑ Dominance   ❑ Steadiness

❑ Influence   ❑ Compliance

4 What personality style would a person most likely have if he or she always began with a warm-up of introductions and/or personal banter before getting to the critical agenda items of a meeting?

❑ Dominance   ❑ Steadiness

❑ Influence   ❑ Compliance

5 What personality style would a person most likely have if he or she stated that the reasons he or she liked a certain product was because it was "new, slick and obviously at the cutting edge"?

❑ Dominance   ❑ Steadiness

❑ Influence   ❑ Compliance

6 What personality style would a person most likely have if he or she provided statistical documentation and backup for every idea he or she presented to the boss?

❑ Dominance   ❑ Steadiness

❑ Influence   ❑ Compliance

(continued)

Test Your DISC Intuitions

7 What personality style would a person most likely have if he or she got upset whenever a meeting was rescheduled at the last minute or called on short notice?

❑ Dominance ❑ Steadiness

❑ Influence ❑ Compliance

8 What personality style would a team member most likely have if he or she insisted that every meeting close with a summary of action items completed and next steps to be done?

❑ Dominance ❑ Steadiness

❑ Influence ❑ Compliance

How did you do? If you are like most people, you marked a relatively even number of questions for each of the four personality styles -- Dominance, Influence, Steadiness and Compliance. A perfect score would have clustered like this:

(next page)

111

Intuitive Answer Sheet

Question Number & Summary	DISC Style
1. Read First then Talk	☑ Compliance
2. Get to the Point	☑ Dominance
3. We've Done it in the Past	☑ Steadiness
4. Warm-Up Needed First	☑ Influence
5. New, Slick, Cutting Edge	☑ Influence
6. Statistical Backup	☑ Compliance
7. Upset by Schedule Changes	☑ Steadiness
8. Actions Completed, Next Steps	☑ Dominance

Some people might want to question or challenge a quiz answer or two. After all, they might argue, there are always areas that are open to multiple interpretations when human behavior is involved. They might also argue that other factors beside personality could be at play – for example prior training or specific events that justified the actions -- which would explain why a person would behave in a certain way.

While such counter-arguments might have merit in particular situations, it's important to remember that we're discussing overall patterns of behavior, here, not isolated instances, and that the personality styles being presented are based on years of empirical research with thousands of subjects. So while there will always be a few exceptions and detours, the DISC personality styles remain a great source for the basic Soft Skills roadmap that we need.

A more detailed explanation of why each question was matched with a corresponding personality style begins just below:

Intuitive Answer Details

1 ☑ Compliance

❖ This person likes to have his or her facts straight, and would rather communicate via reading or writing than through conversation. Has a high need and tolerance for detail, and feels that his/her department members should have those needs and skills, as well.

2 ☑ Dominance

❖ By his or her actions to interrupt, this person is exerting dominance, and because he or she would rather tell than listen, and would rather decide than ponder, he/she wants to get to the key information as quickly as possible.

3 ☑ Steadiness

❖ This person values precedent, repeatability and continuity. As far as he or she is concerned, all methods of doing things should progress on an even track from the past through the present to the future. This is reflected in the way he or she thinks and speaks.

(continued)

Intuitive Answer Details

4 ☑ Influence

❖ This person is people-oriented, and feels that the feelings, moods and well-being of his or her team members are as important as -- if not more important than -- any particular item of business to be transacted.

5 ☑ Influence

❖ In addition to being concerned about people and building consensus, this person likes things that are new and flashy, things that elevate his or her image as being "with it."

6 ☑ Compliance

❖ This person is detail- and information-based in the way he or she makes decisions. He or she "does the homework first," when presenting an idea, and would feel extremely uncomfortable making such a presentation without having the data in hand.

7 ☑ Steadiness

❖ This person values order and progression and reacts negatively to changes and surprises. His or her world works best when it is predictable, and when he/she has ample warning -- and preparation time -- for what comes next.

(continued)

Intuitive Answer Details

8 ☑ Dominance

◈ **This person is motivated by completed tasks and accomplishments. He or she exercises his/her dominance by "insisting" on a summary of action items completed and next steps to be done.**

Is Intuition Enough?

If you find that the DISC system makes intuitive sense to you, then you might be tempted to conclude that having the information already presented here is enough for you to make a determination of a potential hire's Soft Skills, and thus to make a good hiring decision. If that were true, then the relatively large number of people who have already been exposed to DISC on a conceptual basis would be hiring better than their turnover statistics currently indicate that they do.

There are two strong reasons why intuition is not enough:

1. **The basis of personality assessment is mapping how people take in information and make choices and decisions. These processes are largely unconscious, and cannot be identified via conventional interview conversations.**

2. **We are not objective when we hire. We tend to "grade" people high or low depending on whether we like them, and whether we're comfortable with their personality styles. To ask a Hiring Manager with a high "D" personality, for example, to sit still long enough to thoroughly question and record the**

answers of an analytical candidate with a high "C" personality style would be an exercise in futility.

Intuition is not enough. For the reasons mentioned above, we need to use an instrument that is designed to do the information-gathering job for us. And that instrument must be scored and categorized on an objective and systematic basis.

Applying the "Different is Different" Principle

As we begin to think about ways to apply DISC to the world of work, it's very important to understand that there is no hierarchy involved in the assessment of Soft Skills and the assignment of the four personality styles. One style is not better than another. A high "D" personality is not intrinsically more valuable than a high "C". They are different – that's all – simply different. Each style makes its own contribution to keeping our world going.

And in case there is any question, the four personality styles cut across all races, ethnic groups, cultures, religions, heritages and personal orientations. That's why the assessment tools can be validated – they measure factors that are common to humans everywhere, rather than those that tend divide them into separate groups or classes.

The assessment tools are also blind as to a person's age. If you do a DISC Survey on yourself when you are relatively young, and then do it again five, ten or even twenty years later, you will find two things: 1) some slight changes in emphasis may have occurred, based on what you've focused on and learned in the interim; and, 2) uncanny consistency will be apparent in the overall pattern of your scores for Dominance, Influence, Steadiness and Compliance.

So different is different. Contrary to some traditions of management philosophy that have tended to favor one or two personality styles over the others, the wheels of modern commerce would literally grind to a halt if all four DISC styles were not in play in every company every business day.

How important is it to have all four styles working for you? To put the answer into clearer perspective . . .

➤ **Imagine a company which has no one who can make the tough decisions, manage the company's overall resources or focus the enterprise on clear priorities and direction (the _Dominance_ factor);**

-- OR --

➤ **Imagine a company which has no one who can unify and lead teams, build the lasting relationships that create loyal customers, and spur the company forward to adopt new approaches (the _Influence_ factor);**

-- OR --

➤ **Imagine a company which has no one who can take the company's best ideas, products and services and document, systematize and preserve them in a way that reduces wasted effort and prevents the wheels from being reinvented (the _Steadiness_ factor);**

-- OR --

➤ **Imagine a company which has no one who can tackle the company's administrative details, keep the books, collect the money, pay the bills, ensure compliance with laws and regulations and see that quality standards are met (the _Compliance_ factor).**

When you look at it this way, it's virtually impossible to say that any single personality style has more value than another. They are equally important components of the well-oiled machines that we all want our teams, departments and businesses to be.

A Bit of Complication,
But the News Is All Good

It may have already occurred to you that there is no such thing as a person with a "pure" personality – i.e., one that expresses its style along one personality dimension, only. While there are people whose DISC Survey scores are very pronounced in one or two styles, all people have elements of all four styles within them. When you think about it, this is good news in the sense that it means that most of us have a varied repertoire of personality traits to call on to handle the varied tasks that are critical to the performance of our job roles.

But it is also complicated in the sense that some of the people who work for you may have personality styles that seem almost mutually-exclusive – a high "D," for example, who is also a high "C." When you as a Hiring Manager take on the task of matching personality styles to the tasks and roles you want to assign, you may feel at first that the unit or team you're trying to build is a lot more like a complex computer chip than a house of Lincoln Logs.

Fortunately, the DISC system takes this complicating factor into account by measuring *personality style patterns* rather than just the individual styles. Included in the report you receive on each person you assess is a graph that maps all four styles in terms of the relationships between the individual scores. Here are six examples of how the style graphs might look for six different people being tested:

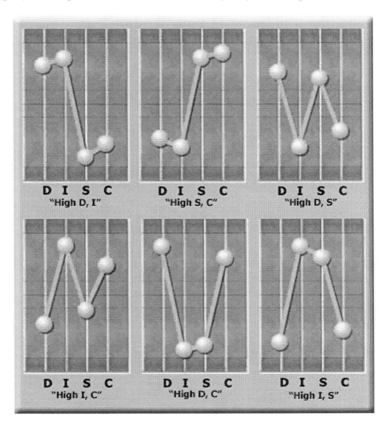

Once you have your results, it's fairly easy to determine whether or not an individual's personality style matches the desired job, role or task by comparing the shape of the style graph to the specifications of the task you want to assign. If, for example, you wanted someone to run your sales department who is self-motivating and projects a commanding presence, who could build and maintain strong relationships with customers and prospects, and could serve as an innovating force within the group, that's someone with a "High D, I" style graph – the top, left graph in the illustration shown above. If the person you are considering for that role has a personality style graph that is similar to the one just to the right of "High D, I", that's someone who scored as a "High S, C" – which is definitely *not* the right set of Soft Skills for the job you want him or her to take on.

In actual practice, it's even easier to make the decision about whether you have a Soft-Skills match than this description makes it sound. Once you know the shape of the style graph you're looking for, little further analysis is necessary. Just look at the shape of the graph of the person you've assessed. It's either close to your target or it's not:

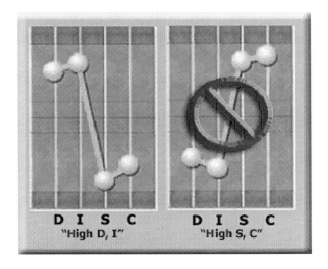

Using Benchmarks

The best way to determine what personality styles you are looking for in a particular position or job role is to use benchmarks. Benchmarks are created by assessing top producers in your department and then working with a DISC professional to use their scores as a template for the ideal hire for that position. Once you have the template, it's an easy matter to compare the results of potential candidates with the template. If your company is too small to provide a basis for comparison, you can work with a DISC professional to select from the classic style graphs for similar job functions and use one of them as your benchmark.

Stress and "Faking" It

One of the most common objections voiced by people who are skeptical about personality assessments is that it's easy to "psych out" the tests. "Once I figure out what qualities my potential employers are looking for," they say, "I can then make the scores come out the way they want." Well, sure they can. Almost anyone can act in a manner that is not really "them" for a short period of time. But what these skeptics may not realize is that the DISC Survey is designed to take such behavior into account – in fact, that it measures such behavior as a part of its normal process.

When you receive your DISC Survey results, you will actually receive two style graphs for each person you assess. The first graph maps the candidate's response to his or her environment, which is also referred to as his or her learned behavior, and the second graph measures his or her natural, or stress behavior.

Why? Most people make an effort to put their "best foot forward" when undergoing a "psychological test," making their selections in a pattern that they feel will be most acceptable in the new situation. This is so common that behavioral researchers are more surprised when it doesn't happen than when it does. Since people are less able to control their "stress" reactions, by measuring both types of behavior, the DISC Survey provides a mechanism for flagging inconsistencies and identifying "faking" behavior.

In the instance where a person with a high "D,I" personality style was applying for a job that required high "S,C" skills, for example, the two graphs might come out something like this:

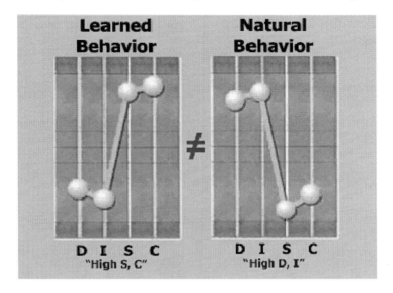

Natural behavior is also called "the true self" because it reflects the way people tend to behave when they are no longer in a "public" setting and the "mask" is off. In the example shown above, the candidate has undergone a crash course of learning new behavior styles in order to get the job. If the candidate does get the job, he or she will be able to "fake it" for a while. When the stress gets high enough, though, this candidate will revert to his or her natural personality style and will no longer be able to tolerate the level of detail and amount of analysis that are required. At that point, the candidate will either become unhappy and leave, or be put on notice and terminated. Either way, it's a bad hire.

Using the DISC Survey to weed out personality mismatches is also beneficial to the potential employee. He or she may not acknowledge it at the time, but the stress of having to work in a job that requires behaviors that are not natural to the employee's personality style will eventually wear him or her down to the point where he or she will "stress out." When that happens, the "wheels will fall off the wagon," and the employee will self-destruct or leave.

In your role as Hiring Manager, here are two things you can do to make sure the wheels don't fall off your wagon:

1. **Deselect those people whose learned and natural DISC style graphs are not congruent with one another; and,**

2. **Make sure the people you hire and who work for you are assigned to tasks that are appropriate to their personality styles.**

The Chemistry of a Great Match

We've all heard of "dream teams," i.e., working groups where the chemistry and fit was so right that it was fun to go to work every day. The quantity and quality of work accomplished by these teams exceeded everyone's expectations. Interpersonal blowups and performance issues were kept to a minimum. The group not only did the work that was assigned to it, but was astonishing in its ability to anticipate and correct potential problems, and actually sought out additional tasks to perform that were not originally defined as part of its mandate.

Whether or not you have personally experienced such a group, I think you would agree that it would be great if more teams and departments actually worked that way. For most of us, achieving that goal seems elusive enough that we tend to think of such teams as rare occurrences, experiences that may happen only once or twice in our careers.

Like great architectural structures, great teams consistently outperform the capabilities of their individual members. These teams do so because of the high degree of match – the chemistry and fit -- between the team members, its leader and the task. These teams are synergetic. They are representations of that magical moment when the whole is greater than the sum of its parts and two plus two equals five.

Can we as Hiring Managers take action to create this kind of synergy, or do we have to wait until it happens by chance? With the kind of information that the DISC Personality Survey puts at our disposal, we *can* make synergy happen. We do this through the hiring selections and task assignments we make, by taking our potential and existing employees' DISC style graphs into account, and by making strong personality matches.

The Manager's Edge

Hiring Managers who become practiced at factoring differences in personality styles into their activities have a definite edge over those who don't. Here are the six major ways they gain their advantage:

Six Advantages - The Manager's Edge	
1	**Managers who assess personality styles as part of their hiring process learn more about the success factors of the candidates they're interviewing, and do a better job of selecting the best.**
2	**Managers who factor personality assessment findings into their team building efforts build teams that function better, and are much more likely to achieve group synergy.**

Six Advantages - The Manager's Edge

3	Managers who apply the four personality styles to their day-to-day interactions with their employees communicate more effectively, and generate fewer misunderstandings.
4	Managers who refer to their employees' style graphs before assigning new tasks and projects are better able to anticipate trouble spots, and have a stronger sense of how hard to push and when to back off.
5	Managers who apply DISC theory to the performance review process do a more complete job of directing and motivating each staff member, and will be seen as being particularly insightful.
6	Managers who share their own DISC findings with new hires once those employees have reported for work will compress the "getting to know you" period for themselves and for their new employees.

Do's and Don'ts of Interacting
With People Every Day

Because the DISC personality styles will give you an insight into how different people think, take in information and communicate, they can serve as a useful format for enhancing your day-to-day interactions with everyone you encounter. In order to use them effectively, you will need to get comfortable enough with the concepts of DISC theory to be able to translate the jargon of the behavioral researcher into the every-day language of normal conversation. This is important because the purpose of using any tool like DISC is to break down barriers, not to create new ones. Here are four do's and don'ts that should help you keep the process within bounds:

Do's and Don'ts of Using DISC	
Do	. . . become familiar enough with the descriptors for each of the four styles that were provided earlier in this chapter that you are unlikely to mistake the characteristics of one style for another.
Don't	. . . do instant "takes" on people. Invest a few minutes in forming a solid impression of the prevailing personality styles they are exhibiting before applying your knowledge of DISC to them.
Do	. . . use the same basic vocabulary you would use in normal conversation. Introduce specific DISC terminology only if you are prepared to get involved in an explanation that will take you off your point.
Don't	. . . play "shrink," or use DISC theory to diminish, limit or entrap people via labels. NEVER say, when challenged by someone, for example, "The reason you can't relate to this is because you're a 'High S'."

Identifying and Communicating
With Each Personality Style

As you go about your daily routine, you will encounter and be challenged to interact with people who possess each of the four DISC styles in a variety of combinations. Every company or team with more than 10 members has all of them. While it is virtually impossible for you to get an exact "take" on a person's personality styles from your intuitive sense of him or her alone, there are some obvious clues that will give you a handle on the prevailing styles of most people you meet, either face-to-face or on the phone. Here are some of the major ones:

(next page)

Clues to Prevailing DISC Styles

D	**In Person:**
	❖ Firm Handshake
	❖ Steady Eye Contact
	❖ Speaks Quickly
	❖ Blunt and to the Point
	❖ Office Décor is Functional
	❖ Desk is Messy
	❖ Dress is Stylish but Functional
	On the Phone:
	❖ Greeting is Clipped but Clear
	❖ Sounds Busy
	❖ Impatient with Warm-Up
	❖ Tendency to Interrupt
	❖ Speaks in Short Sentences
	❖ Blunt and to the Point

(continued)

Clues to Prevailing DISC Styles

In Person:
❖ Double-Clasp Handshake
❖ Warm, Effusive and Chatty
❖ Uses Gestures & Expressions
❖ Initiates Small Talk
❖ Displays Awards and Trophies
❖ Desk is Immaculate
❖ Dress is Fashionable, Showy

On the Phone:
❖ Greeting is Polished & Caring
❖ Open and Friendly Attitude
❖ Responds & Says "Yes" A Lot
❖ Uses Lots of Adjectives
❖ Talks About Feelings
❖ Speaks in Paragraphs

(continued)

Clues to Prevailing DISC Styles

S	## In Person: ◈ Dress is Basic and Casual ◈ Pictures of Family on Walls ◈ Displays Manuals & Files ◈ Conversation Builds Slowly ◈ Asks Questions and Listens ◈ Speaks in Even Tones ◈ Maintains Medium Eye Contact
	## On the Phone: ◈ Greeting is Businesslike ◈ Tends Not to Interrupt ◈ Sounds Sincere ◈ Asks Questions ◈ Speaks Somewhat Slowly ◈ Speaks Diplomatically

(continued)

Clues to Prevailing DISC Styles

C

In Person:
- ❖ Eye Contact is Minimal
- ❖ Handshake is Tentative
- ❖ Casual, Understated Dress
- ❖ Few Gestures & Expressions
- ❖ Desktop is Neat, Orderly
- ❖ Diplomas, Degrees on Walls
- ❖ Requests Documentation

On the Phone:
- ❖ Greeting is Terse
- ❖ Seems Quiet, Non-Responsive
- ❖ Minimal Voice Inflection
- ❖ Answers are Very Short
- ❖ Asks How Things Work
- ❖ Requests Info via Mail/Email

Once you've identified the prevailing DISC style of the person with whom you are communicating, you need to find the best way to speak to that style. To a certain extent, you can "play back" what you are seeing or hearing -- in effect, by mimicking his or her principal style. But be careful, here. If the person you are dealing with knows you, he or she will sense that you are acting out of character. And even if this is your first meeting or phone conversation, the person you're interacting with will probably be quick to sense that something is off-key if you're faking it. It's a little like what happens when you try to adopt the dialect of another part of the country in order to communicate better with someone who lives there. After the first few words, it becomes obvious to the "native" that something is wrong with the structure and cadence of your conversation, and the warning bells start ringing.

Distrust goes way up, trust goes way down, and your position moves rapidly from neutral to negative. For this reason, it's best to speak from your primary style, while making adaptations to account for the style of the person with whom you want to communicate.

Here are some pointers:

Pointers for Positive Communications	
Style	**Pointers**
D	◈ **Keep small talk and warm-up to a minimum.** ◈ **Begin at the end – start by stating the objective of the conversation or meeting, first.** ◈ **Provide one-line answers to questions, but be prepared to provide backup detail if asked.** ◈ **Maintain eye contact, and have answers, when challenged.** ◈ **Summarize and identify next steps, but don't be thrown by a quick decision.**

(continued)

Pointers for Positive Communications

Style	Pointers
I	❖ Warm up the conversation by making a personal comment or two, but weave in your objective as well. ❖ Present what you're working on as a "concept," first – details and objectives later. ❖ Discuss results in terms of their "look" and "feel." ❖ Spark his or her imagination by asking for opinions. ❖ Welcome referrals to others on technical details. Ask for introductions and pointers.
S	❖ Use medium warm up, focusing mainly on his or her work, rather than on his or her surroundings. ❖ Begin by saying you need help in how to make your idea work and whether it fits with current operations. ❖ Emphasize the time spent (if long) working on the project. ❖ Engage him or her by asking for ideas for improvement. ❖ Close by saying you'd like to get back to him or her from time to time to report on progress.

(continued)

Pointers for Positive Communications

Style	Pointers
C	❖ Preface the conversation by saying that it will take just a few minutes. ❖ No warm up – say instead you need help with some data. ❖ Present new documents now, or refer to an existing report. ❖ "C's" love to solve puzzles and problems. Couch your presentations in those terms. ❖ Be prepared for the person to say he or she will need to get back to you, but set a specific time. Follow up promptly.

Using DISC in Crisis Situations

If a crisis occurs, you probably won't have the time to address each person's personality style individually in your team, department or company, at least not right away. Yet you can use DISC theory to construct the best way to speak to the entire group to achieve maximum cooperation to overcome the problem.

There are four dynamics at work in every crisis situation, whether external or internal, physical or fiscal. The first is denial, the second is shock, the third is unity and the fourth is stress. All you have to do to validate these four dynamics is to review the events of 9-11-01 and their aftermath.

As a Hiring Manager, it may become your responsibility to rally the troops and get the group moving in the right direction in a crisis situation. As part of your strategy, you are no doubt going to be called on to hold one or more meetings in order to break through the denial, help people overcome the shock, build unity and deal with the stress. While it is not my intention here to provide you with a complete instruction manual on crisis management, the following four points, which are presented from the viewpoint of DISC theory, should be factored into your thoughts:

1. **Step One** – Breaking through the denial. Before you can effectively rally your troops, you have to get them to face the fact that the problem is real. As a Hiring Manager, you'll be challenged to hold that meeting where the rumors are confirmed or squelched, and the current status of what's known is defined. It's very important that you come to that meeting with all your management and leadership tools at your disposal.

2. **Step Two** -- Dealing with the shock. Shock is the nervous system's response to sudden and intense stress. Physical pain need not be involved. Psychic trauma or catastrophic change is more than enough. The "shock reaction" is a form of paralysis, whether it takes its form as an individual who goes into a coma, or a group of people who sit around, speculate about what's going on, take no action and don't know what to do. Your first objective when dealing with shock must be to put a plan in place to get your people moving again. So during the very first crisis meeting you call, you're going to be challenged to enunciate at least the initial steps of a plan.

3. **Step Three** – Building unity. One thing you may have going in your favor during a time of crisis is that shock often leads to a sense of unity. It's a time when, for a while at least, people put aside their petty differences and work together to overcome a common threat or enemy. As a Hiring Manager, provided that you are not yourself perceived as that threat or enemy, it's an opportunity to get

the group to make strides together that might not otherwise be possible.

4. Step Four – Dealing with the stress. Whether your team or department members will admit it or not, the one thing you can be sure of during a time of crisis is that they will be under stress. As Hiring Manager, this is the time for you to remember that under stress, people revert, or go backwards, to their natural personality styles.

Even though the people in your team or department may be dealing, on the surface, in a manner that seems quite normal, you can assume that the increased stress is in full operation in the zone where their fears and paranoia dwell. Accordingly, they are going to need more than the usual amounts of direction, support and reassurance to function properly.

During those initial crisis meetings you'll be holding, you won't have time to address each person individually. But by taking the four basic personality styles into account, you'll still be able to communicate with them as team members very effectively. As shown in the summary outline presented below dealing with a crisis involving layoffs and economic cutbacks, five concerns are addressed – one that is shared by all team members, and one for each of the four principal personality styles:

(facing page)

Expressed Concern	DISC Style	Underlying Question
1. Will there be more layoffs?	All	Is my job secure?
2. Will we be forced to sacrifice deadlines and quality?	**C**	How much will change?
3. How will we look to the competition?	**I**	Can we still be winners?
4. Will we be required to short-cut our systems and procedures?	**S**	Will we lose continuity?
5. What actions should we take now?	**D**	What's the bottom line?

Selling to Each Personality Style

People with differing personality styles make buying decisions differently, and that is your key to selling to them. This is so whether your sales prospect is an external customer for your products or services, another department head who needs to be convinced about your department's capabilities, or an employee who is having a hard time understanding the value of a new performance standard. The following table will give you a reading of how people with different personality styles make their buying decisions, and how to sell to each:

Selling to the Four Behavior Styles

How they Buy:

◈ Decide Quickly

◈ To Achieve Results

◈ Based on Direct Answers

◈ Based on Seller's Power

◈ Based on Logic and Impressions, Not Details

How to Sell to Them:

◈ Provide Direct Answers

◈ Be Brief and To the Point

◈ Probe using "What?" not "How?"

◈ Don't be Intimidated; Stick to Business

◈ Stress Bottom-Line Benefits

◈ Address Objections Frontally

◈ Close by Providing Options

(continued)

Selling to the Four Behavior Styles

How they Buy:

- ❖ Decide Quickly, Impulsively
- ❖ To Achieve an Upgrade
- ❖ Based on How the Product or Service Looks and Feels
- ❖ Based on Emotion More than Logic
- ❖ Based on Opinions of Others

How to Sell to Them:

- ❖ Provide a Favorable Environment
- ❖ Ask for Input and Opinions
- ❖ Provide Testimonials
- ❖ Share Backup Materials at End
- ❖ To Close, Ask, "How Would this Work for You?"
- ❖ Compliment on His or Her Decision

(continued)

Selling to the Four Behavior Styles

S

How they Buy:
❖ Decide Quickly, Act Slowly
❖ Based on "Fit" with Existing Products or Processes
❖ Based on Comfort with Vendor's Style
❖ Based on Service
❖ Based on Support for Implementation

How to Sell to Them:
❖ Speak Deliberately
❖ Avoid Glib Responses
❖ Provide "How to Use and Implement" Information
❖ Stress Compatibility and Support
❖ Use Collateral Materials to Focus Conversation
❖ To Close, Ask for the Next Step

(continued)

Selling to the Four Behavior Styles

How they Buy:
❖ Decide Slowly
❖ Based on Trust of Vendor
❖ Based on Reliability
❖ Based on External Proof
❖ Based on How the Product Works
❖ Based on Detail

How to Sell to Them:
❖ Speak and Go Slowly
❖ Use Third-Party Proof Sources
❖ Refer to "Reliability Statistics"
❖ Encourage Hands-On Demo's
❖ Provide Backup Info Early
❖ Expect Follow-Ups; Be Punctual
❖ To Close, Ask What Added Data Will Get the Decision Made

To try a demo version of the DISC Personality Survey on for size, go to the next two pages.

(This page intentionally left blank.)

TRY ONE ON FOR SIZE

DISC Personality Survey

If you've never done so before, take this opportunity to sketch a map of your own DISC personality styles. While the questionnaire shown on the following page is a "demo" version of the DISC Personality Survey only, it will give you an initial sense of your major styles. To proceed, follow the instructions provided below.

In the spaces on the facing page, rank the traits listed on each of the 6 lines. Working left to right in each numbered row, you should assign a "4" to the word which is _most like_ you; "3" points to the word that is _like_ you; "2" points to the word that is _somewhat like_ you, and "1" points to the word _least like_ you. Figure your totals for each vertical column and fill in the boxes marked "Total" at the bottom. The combined score of all four vertical columns should equal 60.

DISC Personality Survey (Demo Version Only)

EXAMPLE

#	1 Competitive	2 Inspiring	3 Steady	4 Cautious
	Column 1	Column 2	Column 3	Column 4
1)	___ Competitive	___ Inspiring	___ Steady	___ Cautious
2)	___ Self Certain	___ Optimistic	___ Deliberate	___ Exacting
3)	___ Adventurous	___ Enthusiastic	___ Friendly	___ Logical
4)	___ Decisive	___ Flexible	___ Patient	___ Strict
5)	___ Assertive	___ Impulsive	___ Stabilizing	___ Precise
6)	___ Vigorous	___ Responsive	___ Sympathetic	___ Factual
#	___ TOTAL D	___ TOTAL I	___ TOTAL S	___ TOTAL C

staffdynamics
workforce performance specialists

Circle the highest total and note which letter appears in the box with your highest. (Either D, I, S or C) *For demo purposes only!*

To determine your principal personality style, take a look at the highest numeric score you generated. If it's greater than 16, it's considered to be "high," with scores of 20 or above being placed in the "highest" range. Likewise, scores of less than 14 are considered "low," with scores of 10 or below being placed in the "lowest" range.

How did you do? Are you a high "D", an "I", an "S", or a "C"? If you factor the "minimum-high" number of 16 into the equation, do you have two "high," and two "low" DISC styles? Both of these occurrences are very usual. If you scored "high" on three of the four styles, you are part of a slightly smaller group, but are still a part of the statistical mainstream.

If your personality scores on this demo assessor are a little surprising to you, let the findings "sit" for a while before making your final judgment. Remember that this "demo model" is not the full assessor, and that the exercise was presented to you to give you a taste of the process rather than to generate a final, 'scientific' rendering. So it could be that if you took the full DISC Survey, your style graph would come out differently.

Or maybe the demo assessment is pretty close, and your consternation is based on the fact that it's a lot easier to apply DISC theory to the behavior patterns of others than it is to apply it to yourself. That's why you need to give it some time, to see what insights it brings to the surface.

However you scored and however you feel about it, you're not alone. As the percentages shown earlier in this chapter demonstrate, the four personality styles distribute themselves fairly evenly across the population. You are also in very distinguished company. Here are examples of some other people with high "D's," "I's," "S's" and "C's":

Welcome to the Club!

Style	Person
D	❖ Bill O'Reilly ❖ Donald Trump ❖ George Washington ❖ Hillary Clinton ❖ Martha Stewart ❖ Michael Jordan
I	❖ Bill Clinton ❖ Mohammed Ali ❖ Oprah Winfrey ❖ Princess Diana Robin Williams ❖ Ronald Reagan
S	❖ Tom Brokaw ❖ Laura Bush ❖ George Harrison ❖ Barbara Bush ❖ Walter Cronkite ❖ Dwight Eisenhower
C	❖ William Greenspan ❖ Michael Dell ❖ Bill Gates ❖ Diane Sawyer ❖ Ted Koppel ❖ Barbra Streisand

Unleashing the Power

Whether the team you are building is comprised of you and just one other person, or the entire staff of your company, you can tap more of the power of its members by factoring both their Hard Skills and their Soft Skills into your decisions. DISC theory and the DISC Personality Survey can help you do this, by giving you a handle on how personality styles operate, and a yardstick by which to measure them.

Using these tools, the key to your success is not so much what you add to the mix as what you take out. When you deselect people whose style graphs are incongruent, you defuse the ticking time bombs. And when you build teams that match people with tasks based on their personality styles as well as their technical abilities, you eliminate another built-in source of stress. That combination alone will free up much more of the energy of your team to focus on the task at hand, unleashing a level of power that is awesome to behold.

DISC Elevator Music

To sharpen your understanding of DISC theory, it's fun sometimes to apply the four personality styles to the details of daily life. Imagine, for example, four people who have just boarded the car of a brand-new elevator.

They don't know each other, but each person has a different personality style. For the purposes of this mental exercise, imagine there's a "D," an "I," an "S" and a "C" in the group. Here's how the story would unfold:

❖ **The "High D" will jostle to get in first and position him or herself where he or she can control all the buttons. You'll notice that he or she is in a hurry.**

❖ **The "High I" will stand where he or she can see everyone, and will begin working the crowd before the door even closes. He/she likes the new, fancy elevator design.**

❖ The "High S" will feel a little disoriented by this new-fangled contraption. He or she will be eyeballing the others to make sure they all get in safely.

❖ The "High C" will stand away from the group, so he or she can minimize contact with the others three. He or she will be looking for the inspection sticker -- to make sure the elevator conforms to safety standards.

Chapter Take-Aways

Item	Idea, Issue or Action Item	Done / Noted
1	Learn more about DISC theory -- Dominance, Influence, Steadiness and Compliance – and how it applies to my situation.	☐
2	Take the full DISC Personality Survey and study the reports. Clarify what my results mean by asking questions.	☐
3	Bring the DISC Personality Survey in-house and build a benchmark around my _____ best _____.	☐
4		☐
5		☐
6		☐
7		☐

Note: The purpose of this "Take-Away" page is to encourage you to summarize the key points of the materials you've read in this Chapter. To get the process started, I have listed three items that I feel are important, but this list is not exhaustive.

Take this opportunity to inventory what you've learned and crystallize what you want to implement before moving on.

Chapter Six

Hiring
Winners

L ike many management processes in business, hiring right has goals that are easy to articulate, but which are escorted by a series of steps that are a bit more challenging to implement. In this Chapter, we'll address both the goals and the steps. We'll begin by formulating the overall goals of the hiring process we want to create. Then we'll define the necessary hiring steps to convert the theories into action. Along the way, we'll present how the steps contribute to the overall goals, and we'll provide specific pointers on how to put those steps into practice.

Initial Goals and Objectives of Hiring Right

Here are five goals and seven objectives of hiring right:

Goals and Objectives of Hiring Right	
A. Goals -- We want to create a recruiting and hiring process which:	
1	Empowers us to identify and attract the best talent for the position.
2	Enables us to determine and evaluate those candidates' Hard Skills and Soft Skills (i.e., Can-Do and Will-Do factors).
3	Allows us to anticipate which of the candidates will be the most successful.
4	Informs us as to which of the Candidates will do best at which kinds of tasks.
5	Helps us judge which of the Candidates are most likely to be long-term players.

Goals and Objectives of Hiring Right

B. Objectives -- By implementing this recruiting and hiring process, we want to:

1	Attract and motivate active interest and pursuit by the highest-quality candidates.
2	Sell those candidates on the positive reasons for working with us.
3	Disqualify candidates more quickly who do not meet our standards.
4	Identify and hire the best people and create strong bonds and working relationships with them.
5	Generate a positive "buzz" in the marketplace about working for our company.
6	Renew the enthusiasm and commitment or our existing staff.
7	Operate within time frames that enhance our competitive edge.

Preparing the Way:
Magnetizing the Recruiting & Hiring Process

You'll notice that several of the items in the lists of goals and objectives shown on the pages above focus on "attracting" candidates or creating a "buzz" in the marketplace or on "selling" the candidate on the benefits of working for your company. Even though many people conceive of hiring right as a process of eliminating unqualified candidates (or alternatively, selecting the most qualified candidates), this is really not the first step. To be effective, the message your recruiting and hiring process sends out to the world must be compelling enough to attract top talent. To be compelling, it must begin with an invitation. Before a candidate can be properly interviewed and qualified for your position, he or she must be interested enough in pursuing that position to be motivated to go through your qualifying steps.

This is especially so for those candidates who are successfully employed – yet are dissatisfied and open to other options – in their current positions. If your hiring process does not appeal to these types of candidates, then a majority of the candidates who do respond may not be of the caliber you desire. And if that's the case, your screening and interviewing process will succeed only in boiling the group of candidates who do respond down to the best of a rather bland bunch.

These may sound like harsh words, and perhaps they are. But they describe the real experiences of many Hiring Managers who enter the competitive fray of recruiting and hiring without the proper tools to attract the kinds of people to work for them who could really make a difference to their company.

What can you do to magnetize top talent? Here are three areas where a little preparation by you and your staff can go a long way toward assembling the right competitive tools and increasing the magnetism of your hiring process.

(facing page)

Magnetizing the Hiring Process

Step:	Description:
One	Strip away the barriers to hiring top people -- in your advertising, paperwork requirements and offer timing.
Two	Create a positive and consistent recruiting and hiring message.
Three	Involve and energize your staff to help you by developing selling points of the opportunity and empowering them to generate referrals.

Here are the details that accompany those three steps:

Step One Details:

STEP ONE in magnetizing the recruiting and hiring process is to *strip away the barriers to attracting the best talent.* Here are three prime examples of barriers – some of which have been discussed in earlier Chapters -- that can be stripped away at no additional cost and can have a momentous impact on your efforts to attract the best possible people to your opportunity:

A. **Recruiting advertisements** that stress what skills and experience levels the candidate MUST HAVE to qualify for the position while saying nothing about what the candidate WILL ENJOY.

B. **Interview meetings for experienced candidates** who are currently employed which begin by requiring them fill out lengthy job application forms in the personnel office prior to meeting anyone in the department.

C. **Hiring processes that take too long** from first interview to offer decision, as time kills all deals.

Here's what you need to do to strip those barriers away:

A. **Review and Revise Your Recruitment Ads**: Make sure the advertisements you run for the people you want to hire are positive and not defensive. This means that those ads should be composed of four types of information, only:

1. A brief description of the company, the job and its key duties and responsibilities;

2. A section on what the successful candidate will enjoy – i.e., the positive selling points of the company and the job;

3. To the extent that you feel compelled to include requirements, or "must-have's" in an ad, do it subtly, positioning those requirements in the background rather than as the main point – for example, "apply your skill and experience as a certified broker to one of the . . ." is a much more inviting statement than, ". . . you must have full certification as a broker to be considered . . ."; and,

4. An action statement that defines the next step to be taken by the potential candidate.

B. **Put the Paperwork in its Proper Place** – Design your hiring process so that the experienced candidate is welcomed first, before being asked to complete detailed, job-application paperwork. If your Human Resources department insists that the paperwork must be filled out early in the process, meet and greet the candidate when he or she comes in for his or her first interview and escort him/her to the proper area to get it done. This simple practice will go a long way toward making the candidate feel welcome and comfortable.

C. **Expedite the Offer Decision** – Make a list of the steps that your company takes from first interview to offer decision, identifying any bottlenecks and streamlining, eliminating or working around them. For example, if the process requires multiple interviews, find ways to bunch-schedule them so that they can be accomplished within 5-7 business days. If testing or personality assessment is involved, administer the tests soon enough that you can get a jump on the scoring for your semi-finalists. Begin conducting your reference checks on your finalists early enough to complete them in time for the decision deadline.

Step Two Details:

STEP TWO is to *work with your staff and key managers to make sure your overall recruiting and* *hiring message is positive and consistent.* All of the participants in the hiring process will play key roles in qualifying. To make that process magnetic, work with them to do two additional things as well:

A. **Develop and Adopt a USP** – or Unique Selling Proposition -- for your company and the opportunities it provides. This can be as simple as a 30-second presentation of the positives of what makes your company stand out.

The power of this USP is not so much that it is comprehensive, as that it captures your company's unique advantages.

Make your USP brief and memorable. The selling points you developed for your recruitment ad are a great place to start. If every person on your team uses this USP as his or her starting point in describing the opportunity to the candidates interviewed without sounding canned or over-rehearsed, then the sense of unity this conveys will itself exert an additional magnetic force.

B. **Get Everyone Prepared to Answer this Key Question** -- "Why should I work for your company?" -- any time it comes up during the interview process.

The question actually takes two forms:

- For the active (and most likely unemployed) job seeker, it is, "Why should I *choose your company over another?*"; and,
- For the recruited candidate who is comfortably (if not happily) employed, the question is, "Why should I *quit my job and go to work for your company (over another)?*"

When you prepare yourself and your staff to answer both of these questions effectively, your competitive position improves noticeably.

The focus of STEP TWO is to involve your team by having them play a key role in attracting top talent to your organization, NOT to create a uniform and mechanized response. To the contrary, you *want* each member of your team to express these positives in his or her own terms. By starting with a USP that has been generated and adopted by the group, you will have defined a common theme and starting point from which each individual can diverge and express his or her own variations and style.

Step Three Details:

STEP THREE in magnetizing your hiring process is to *brief your staff on the key requirements of the position(s) to be filled and to brainstorm with them about what the successful candidate will enjoy.* This activity is different from developing your USP, in that it focuses on the benefits and selling points of your particular job offering and of working for your department, rather than on those of the company as a whole. Your objective here is to *energize your staff about the opportunity and to impel them to provide you with referrals of potential candidates.*

This is a very important step that can save you a great deal of time and money. Meet with your group face-to-face, using memo's and written reminders as follow up devices, only.

Encourage your staff to ask their friends and associates whom they know who might be qualified. In effect, you're asking them to talk up the opportunity outside the company, and to create a "buzz" in the local community, as well as through their personal and professional associations and spheres of influence. In order to command the attention of your staff and to stimulate referrals, offering a referral bonus is a great idea. Just make sure that the rewards are keyed to successful hires (for example, a $1,000^{00} bonus that is paid to the referring employee in two

installments -- $500^{00} to be paid 60 days after the candidate has been hired and is still on board, and $500^{00} to be paid 120 days after the candidate's start date).

And whether you offer a bonus or not, see to it that both the person who makes the referral that results in the hire, and the person who contributes the largest number of useful referrals overall, both receive public praise for their efforts.

When you succeed in magnetizing your hiring process, you make your job as Hiring Manager much easier. For when great candidates WANT to work for your company or department, then you are really in a position to select from the best. And when you involve your staff in the process of defining your USP and the selling points of the opportunities being offered, you gain three advantages over your competition:

1. **You'll have a unified team communicating a consistent message to every candidate you meet;**

2. **By giving your team members a stake in the recruiting and hiring process, you will heighten their commitment to help the new hire(s) succeed; and,**

3. **By asking them to help you articulate the positive aspects of working for your department and company, you'll foster an environment where they'll resell themselves on the value of *their* decisions to work for you as well.**

Inviting In Versus Screening Out

The points that have been made in the section just above are much more important than they might seem at first glance, as they concern the posture you take in your recruiting and hiring efforts and thus lay the groundwork and set the tone for all that follows. As someone who has watched many companies make the same mistakes over and over again and waste millions of dollars in recruitment advertising during my fifteen-year tenure in the Search and Staffing industry, it boggles my mind how often Hiring Managers seem to forget or ignore these all-important first principles of recruiting:

(next page)

First Principles of Recruiting

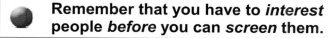

To attract the best, issue an invitation, first.

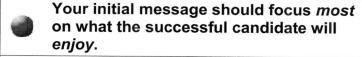

Remember that you have to *interest* people *before* you can *screen* them.

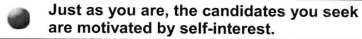

Your initial message should focus *most* on what the successful candidate will *enjoy*.

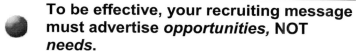

Just as you are, the candidates you seek are motivated by self-interest.

To be effective, your recruiting message must advertise *opportunities,* NOT *needs.*

The Hiring and Selection Process: An Overview

Once we have put the tools into place to attract the caliber of candidate we want, we have reached the point where our hiring and selection process comes into play. As we discussed in some detail in *Chapter Two -- We Hire for Skills, Fire for Personality,* that hiring process must be systematic and consistent, and must be designed to make sure we gather enough of the right information to achieve a balanced view of each candidate's Hard Skills and Soft Skills, technical talents and personality characteristics, before making our final selection.

We do this in order to select people who not only exhibit the "Can-Do's" to do the job in the short run, but who also have the "Will-Do's" – i.e., the motivation and interpersonal abilities -- to fit in with the team and make a long-term contribution to the company. In addition to assessing both Hard and Soft Skills, we also want a hiring and selection process that helps us avoid the eleven *Hiring Blunders* detailed in Chapter Four.

Here's an overview of the process that meets these multiple requirements:

Hiring and Selection Overview

Step	Title	Addresses
# 1	Candidate Identification	Approaching and using multiple sources for identifying potential candidates; how to prioritize those sources for optimum results.
# 2	Telephone Interview	Using the phone as the first tool in identifying / qualifying most potential candidates; what questions to ask and areas to probe.
# 3	1st Face-to-Face Interview	Pacing and timing, what items to explore, selling versus qualifying, how to leave things with the candidate.

(continued)

Hiring and Selection Overview

Step	Title	Addresses
# 4	DISC Personality Survey	Best use of assessment tools like DISC, how to describe them to the candidate, how to interpret the results.
# 5	1st Evaluation	How to approach this first go/no go decision point; the value of a "homework" assignment for candidates who "pass go" and make it to the next step.
# 6	2nd Face-to-Face Interview	What to cover; handling negatives; how to balance "Can-Do's" and "Will-Do's;" first steps to avoid offer-time surprises.
# 7	Reference Checks, 2nd Evaluation	Who to call; what to ask; how many references you need; factoring in the DISC Survey findings; using an evaluation checklist.
# 8	Pre-Hire Interview	Floating an offer and addressing concerns; start-readiness; resignation drill.

(continued)

Hiring and Selection Overview

Step	Title	Addresses
# 9	Offer, Hire, Pre-Start Assignment & Start	Offer presentation and acceptance; actions to reinforce the candidate's decision to go to work for you; tips on how to help him or her make it unscathed through the resignation.
# 10	New Hire Paperwork	Making sure that all of the administrative necessities are handled and the decks are cleared for the new hire.

Here's how these hiring steps look as a flow chart:

(next page)

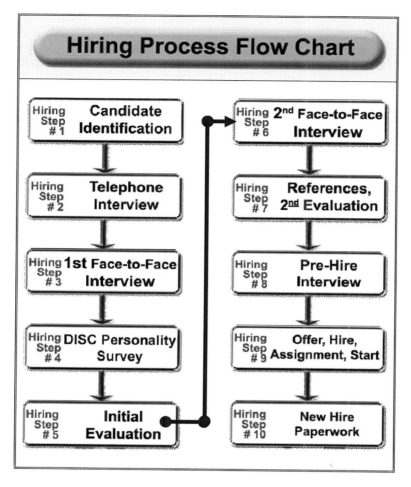

Take a moment to review this flow chart prior to moving on. It's your roadmap to hiring right. We'll be referring to it often as we provide detailed explanations, how-to's, guidelines and pointers for each of the ten hiring steps.

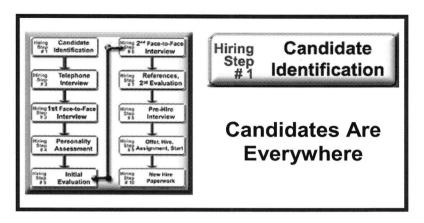

In today's world of electronically-interconnected everything and the emergence of Internet-based job boards, your first impulse in identifying potential candidates for your openings most probably will be to go on line. While the Internet can be a useful source of the potential candidates you need, it does have its drawbacks, and is certainly not the first place you should go to find them. Here are three reasons why not:

A. Even if you find people there whose resumes indicate they are a perfect technical match for the job being offered, they are still "wild cards" at this point in the process – i.e., you know nothing about them, and no person has referred them to you whom you trust.

B. You will invariably be inundated by multitudes of "wannabe's" who have used "agents" to set their job board listings to respond automatically to any job posting that meets certain, often very general, criteria. You may find that fewer than one in one hundred of these respondents have the skills and experience that are in the ballpark of the requirements of your position, and that an even lower percentage qualify when you factor in geography and money.

C. High-demand candidates on the 'net are generally swamped with opportunities from recruiters and from other companies. Given the number of competing interviews and offers that will inevitably surround them, your odds of actually hiring one of these folks from this source are greatly diminished.

For these reasons, Internet recruiting has an important place in your sourcing list, but its position on that list should not be number one. What you should do instead is to generate and work through a list of sources that moves from "known" sources to "unknown" sources in systematic fashion, thus taking advantage of work you've done and contacts you've made in the past, first, and moving to the "unknown" sources only if the known sources prove unfruitful.

Here's a list of sources of potential candidates that has been arranged in tiers that move from those that are "known" to those that are "unknown:"

Prioritized List of Sources

Tier	Descriptions & Comments
1	**Referrals:** • **From Internal Job Postings** • **From Colleagues** • **From Employees** • **From Previous Employers and Employees** • **From Vendors** • **From Professional Associations** • **From previous Applicants** • **From Special Interest Groups (i.e., AARP)** • **From Trade Schools or University Department Heads** • **From In-House Recruiters**

Prioritized List of Sources

Tier	Descriptions & Comments
1	**Comments on Referrals:** • The main advantage of starting with referrals is that each of them will be targeted in the sense that each referral source knows enough about you or your industry to have a sense what specific types of candidates to suggest. • Referrals also come with an "intro" and a built-in reference – i.e., the person providing the referral should be able to give you some perspective on the person being referred.
2	**Targeted Job Fairs, Open Houses or Discovery Sessions:** • If the job fair is conducted properly, you or someone you know will have had the opportunity to observe and speak with the person referred before passing him or her on to you.

(continued)

Prioritized List of Sources

Tier	Descriptions & Comments
3	**Internal Resume File or Database:** • Whether they come from your own files or a computerized company database, resumes of candidates and applicants from prior hiring activities can be a great source for candidates for this one, particularly if the person you're contacting felt like he or she was treated respectfully last time around. • And even if the person you contact is currently situated and not looking to move, he or she may know someone who is right for your opportunity today.
4	**Specialist Search and Generalist Staffing Firms:** • If your need is for professional-level staff or managers with specialized skills and knowledge, specialized search firms are often your most effective source. • If your need is for clerical staff, telemarketers, inside sales people, customer service rep's, lower-level accounting or computer support staff, or light industrial workers or supervisors, generalist staffing firms can be an excellent source.

Prioritized List of Sources

Tier	Descriptions & Comments
5	**Classified Ads and Internet Job Postings:** • While classified ads and Internet postings are merging to some degree in the major newspapers, don't forget the smaller publications and business journals in your locale. The cost is much lower to advertise in those periodicals and they are sometimes quite effective. • If the timing works out, an ad in the local newsletter for your professional association may be your best advertising investment of all.
6	**College Recruitment:** • While University department heads may be a good source of referrals for experienced candidates, if you have a need for interns or entry-level candidates, college recruitment may be your best way to go. • If you use local colleges and universities, this need not be an expensive proposition.

Prioritized List of Sources

Tier	Descriptions & Comments
7	**Internet Resume Database Search:** • This resource tends to promise more than it delivers, for three reasons: 1. Can be very time-consuming; 2. Too many wannabe's; and, 3. High-demand candidates are overexposed and thus very difficult to hire.
8	**Walk-Ins:** • Make sure to monitor job seekers who seek your company out, but don't depend on this as a prime source of candidates when you have an opening. • If your profession is sales-related, pay special attention to the good sales people who manage to penetrate your reception screen and meet with you. One of them may be your next hire.

While your initial recruiting message will be the same as you reach out to these sources, your tactical approach will be a little different for each of them. This is because each type represents a different constituency, audience or setting, and each will be motivated by self-interests that are somewhat unique. Here are some pointers on how to approach each of the eight categories:

Pointers on Approaching Sources

 ## 1.) <u>Referrals</u>:

❖ Your key for gathering useful referrals from almost any referring source is to interest that person enough in the prospective opportunity that he or she will actually stop and think for a few moments about what you're asking, and then to focus that thinking on the basic parameters of the position you're trying to fill.

❖ Here are the steps:

A. Prepare a very short version of your recruiting message that contains two or three basic qualifying requirements and at least three items the successful candidate would enjoy.

B. Express the qualifying requirements in terms of "can-do's" rather than "must-haves."

C. When asking for referrals, use a phrase like, "I was wondering who you know *who could handle* an opportunity such as this," rather than ". . . *who is looking.*" This will allow you to cast a wider net, as your referring source is probably not privy to the day-to-day job aspirations of more than a very small percentage of the qualified people he or she knows.

D. If your referral source says he or she would like to "think about" your request and call you back, set a time when you can call him or her back instead.

Pointers on Approaching Sources

E. After getting the necessary contact information on a referral, ask, "Why do you think _____ would be good for this situation?" Listen carefully to the response.

F. When you get the first referral, don't stop. Ask, "Who else do you know who could handle such an opportunity?"

G. Whether you get a useful referral or not, thank your source for his or her time in working with you.

 ## 2.) <u>Targeted</u> <u>Job</u> <u>Fairs</u>, <u>Open</u> <u>Houses</u> or <u>Discovery</u> <u>Sessions</u>:

<u>First</u>, <u>some</u> <u>definitions</u>:

❖ A <u>Job Fair</u> is an event sponsored by a third party where you rent booth space and use the crowd flow as a way to gather resumes and meet candidates.

❖ An <u>Open House</u> is an event sponsored by your company, usually held at your facility, where potential candidates can bring their resumes and meet you and your staff. An informal, welcoming presentation is usually included.

❖ A <u>Discovery Session</u> or <u>Career Night</u> is an event sponsored by your company, held in a neutral, off-site venue, involving a formal presentation, a question-and-answer period, and the opportunity for a short interview for each interested participant. This is a useful method

Pointers on Approaching Sources

for attracting and pre-screening candidates where sales, customer service or interpersonal skills are more important to the hire than specific industry knowledge. Note: If you feel the term, "Career Night," is overused; try something like, "Discovery Session," instead.

Your first objective:

❖ For a Job Fair, it is to attract a significant portion of the traffic flow to your booth. One of the most effective ways to do that is to conduct a drawing for a prize that would be of interest to your audience (like a software package or PDA), with the cost of entry being a resume or business card and, if you request, a five-minute interview.

❖ In the case of the Open House or Discovery Session, your first objective is to "fill the hall." Do this through a combination of advertising and pro-active telephone and email invitations to "likely suspects" from your resume database files.

What to do next:

❖ Stand up and work the crowd. Shake hands. Make sure every participant is welcomed. Gather resumes and cards and conduct Micro-Interviews.

❖ Observe the participants carefully. Schedule follow-ups with those who are the most promising.

Pointers on Approaching Sources

 ### 3.) <u>Internal</u> <u>Resume</u> <u>File</u> <u>or</u> <u>Database</u>:

❖ If possible, begin the conversation with some reference to the last contact that you or someone in your company had with this individual.

❖ Say something like, "_____, you and I spoke on ___(date)___ about _____,

and while your skills did not quite match our specific needs at that time, I'm working on something now that may be more appropriate. Have I caught you a moment when you are free to talk?"

❖ Even if you are dead certain that this person has the hard skills you seek, make an approach that is a bit indirect or circumspect, asking more for referrals and thoughts than if the prospect is interested. This is for two reasons:

A. You will be in a better negotiating position with the prospect as the process unfolds if he or she volunteers his or her interest, first; and,
B. It's very likely that most of the people you call will not be interested for themselves – thus, your focus on referrals will be both appropriate and more fruitful if you introduce that idea in the beginning of the conversation.

Pointers on Approaching Sources

❖ Say, "We're currently searching for a _____(title)_____ who can _____, _____ and _____, working in an environment where successful performance could lead to _____, _____ and _____. Who do you know who could handle an opportunity such as this?"

❖ If the prospect says, "I might be interested," say, "Tell me some more about your qualifications."

❖ If the prospect says, "I can't think of anyone," say, "who comes to mind from your last job, or from your professional contacts?"

❖ If the prospect says, "I'll have to think it over and get back to you," say, "Great -- I appreciate that! As I said, the requirements are _____, _____ and _____, and the opportunities are _____, _____ and _____. When in the next couple of days would be a good time for me to call you back?"

4.) Specialist Search and Generalist Staffing Firms:

❖ Selecting the right firm for the job you need to fill is of paramount importance. While some firms will purport to be able to handle every level and specialty, that claim is mostly untrue. To help with the selection process, ask for a firm's "Has Done's" as well as its "Can Do's."

❖ To motivate these firms to give your needs their highest-priority attention, focus on:

A. Access – demonstrate that you will respond to their referrals and will provide timely

Pointers on Approaching Sources

feedback on candidates submitted and interviewed.

B. Selling Points – work with the firm you select to develop a well-substantiated list of reasons why candidates should want to work for your company.

C. Payment – do the internal homework necessary to ensure timely payment of fees.

❖ To ensure the referrals you receive from them are on the mark, work on:

A. Specifications – make sure the job requirements are nailed down and clearly stated and understood.

B. Talent Sources – Give specific examples of the types of companies that generate the talent that you seek, perhaps providing abstracted thumbnail sketches of your own most recent successful hires.

(continued)

Pointers on Approaching Sources

5. Classified Ads and Internet Job Postings:

◈ Remember to implement ads that conform to the four criteria listed in the section on "Magnetizing the Hiring Process," above:

A. A brief <u>description of the job</u> and its key duties and responsibilities;

B. A section on what the successful candidate will <u>enjoy</u> – i.e., the positive selling points of the job;

C. A brief <u>section on requirements</u>, positioned as background information rather than as the ad's prime content (i.e., "apply your skill and experience as a certified broker to one of the . . ." rather than, ". . . you must have full certification as a broker to be considered . . ."

D. An <u>action statement</u> that defines the next step to be taken by the potential candidate.

◈ Establish a procedure that handles and routes ad response appropriately and quickly.

◈ Have an alternative strategy in place in case the ads do not pull the response you need.

(continued)

Pointers on Approaching Sources

 ### 6.) <u>College</u> <u>Recruitment</u>:

❖ If yours is a more general need, i.e., for interns, entry-level sales or customer service hires, arrange to stage events like the Open Houses or Discovery Sessions described above. This way you can present your opportunity in concept and in detail, while observing the students in group- and one-on-one settings, prior to committing to formal interviews.

 ### 7.) <u>Internet</u> <u>Resume</u> <u>Database</u> <u>Search</u>:

❖ Your approach to people whose resumes you find on the Internet – whether you find them on job sites or via search engines – should be similar to the one you use for prospects from your internal files, with two important differences:

A. Your introductory statements should refer to the source where you found each prospect, i.e., "_____, my name is _____ _____ and I am __(title)__ for __(company)__. I recently found your resume on __(Job Board or search engine)__, and given your background, I thought it would be worth our while to talk for a few minutes. Have I reached you at a time when you can speak freely?"

Pointers on Approaching Sources

B. Because many of these people will have been overexposed, you should focus your expectations on using your contacts with them as a basis for gathering referrals.

 ### 9.) <u>Walk-Ins</u>:

❖ Information on any walk-ins who contacted your company prior to your current search would have been referred to your company resume database files, as addressed in source item # 3, above.

❖ For walk-ins who appear during the course of your search, careful screening is the key. Here's how to handle them:

A. Brief your reception staff that while interviews are by appointment only (as always), to be on the lookout for people whose resumes contain the key (hard) skill sets you seek.

B. Instruct the reception staff that if a likely prospect appears, to bring the resume to you while the prospect is still there:

➢ If the background looks promising and you have the time, walk out and greet the prospect, asking him or her a few initial questions about qualifications and reasons for seeking a position, and explain that a full interview would still have to be by appointment.

➢ If the prospect is interesting enough to warrant an interview, schedule one right

Pointers on Approaching Sources

there, or get a list of times from the prospect when he or she could be available. If appropriate, ask the prospect to complete any necessary job application paperwork before he or she leaves.

➢ If the prospect is of little or marginal interest right now, thank him or her for his or her interest, and say you'll get back to him or her, if appropriate, as the interview process develops.

C. Instruct your reception staff that if the walk-in candidate does not seem to be a likely prospect, to gather the resume, thank him or her for his or her interest, and to say that someone will get back to him or her, if appropriate, as the process unfolds.

Pre-Screening:
Resumes, Voicemail and Micro-Interviews

Some of the sourcing techniques mentioned in the pointers table just above may generate such a large number of prospective candidates that some sort of initial screening method will be needed to prevent the hiring process from getting bogged down by the sheer numbers of respondents. If your recruiting efforts are as successful as you would like them to be, this will be particularly true for Internet-based resumes, Classified and Job Board Ad responses, Open House and Discovery Sessions and, to a lesser extent, Walk-Ins.

While it is beyond the scope of this book to provide a catalogue of all of the methods you can use to pre-screen prospective candidates, here's a primer that will help you with four major pre-screening issues:

Primer on Pre-Screening

Issue # I:

Too Many Internet-Based Resumes

1. Your Objective:

  ➢ To decide whether to include this prospective candidate in your interviewing / hiring process (first step: telephone interview).

2. Preparation:

  ➢ Determine 2 – 4 "Can-Do" Factors (or search keys or key words) that would determine whether the prospective candidate would make the initial "cut."

3. Electronic Resume Subset Search:

  ➢ Enter the "Can-Do" factors into the search engine and run them against the assembled group of resumes.

  ➢ If this search yields too few results, delete the least important of your key words from the search engine criteria and run the search again. Continue this process until you have a group of manageable size.

4. **Manual Scan and Sort:**

> ➢ Scan the resulting resumes manually, spending no more than 30 seconds on each.

> ➢ Look for: verification of "Can-Do's," acceptable geography and money, if available.

> ➢ Based on this scan, sort the resumes into two piles:

>> A. May BE the person I'm looking for;
>> B. May KNOW the person I'm looking for (referrals).

> ➢ Call the prospective candidates in the "A" pile, first.

Issue # II:

Too Many File-Based Resumes

1. **Your Objective:**

> ➢ To decide whether to include this prospective candidate in your interviewing / hiring process (first step: telephone interview).

2. **Preparation:**

> ➢ Determine 2 – 4 "Can-Do" Factors (or search keys or key words) that would determine whether or not the prospective candidate would make the initial "cut."

3. **Manual Resume Subset Search**

> ➢ Using the two most important "Can-Do's," go through the pile of resumes manually, spending no more than 15 seconds on each one.

➤ Scan for compliance with the "Can-Do's," sorting the resumes into two piles:

    A. HAS the "Can-Do's"
    B. DOES NOT HAVE the "Can-Do's"

➤ Discard pile "B."

4. Manual Scan and Sort:

➤ Scan the "A" pile manually, devoting no more than 20 seconds to each resume.

➤ Look for: detail on "Can-Do's," acceptable geography and money, if available.

➤ Based on this scan, sort the resumes into two piles:

    A. May BE the person I'm looking for;
    B. May KNOW the person I'm looking for (referrals).

➤ Call the prospective candidates in the "A" pile first.

Issue # III:

How to Handle a High Volume of Calls From People Who Want To Register for An Open House or Discovery Session

1. Your Objectives:

➤ To determine how many people are planning to attend the event.

➤ To make sure the best prospective candidates do attend.

2. **Modify Your Ad Action Statement:**

   ➤ When advertising your Open House or Discovery Session, write an action statement that says something like this: "To Register, please give us a call at (___) ___ - ____." (Use a direct dial number or extension.)

3. **Create a Voice-Mail Message that Addresses these Four Points:**

   ➤ Thank you for responding to the (Open House or Discovery Session) for ___(company)___ .

   ➤ We will make every effort to return your call in the next 48 hours.

   ➤ In the meantime, after the beep, please leave a 30-second message summarizing:

   - Your current work and industry background;
   - Why you are interested in attending this (Open House or Discovery Session); and,
   - Three adjectives that best describe your approach to your work.

   ➤ In case we can't reach you, please consider the message you leave as your registration for this (Open House or Discovery Session), which, as you know, is being held at the _____ from ____ to ____ PM.

4. **Monitor the Responses Carefully:**

   ➤ You'll be amazed at the range of responses you'll receive, everything from lengthy monologues to silent hang-ups. You'll also get some well-crafted, crisp presentations from people who are clearly skilled at communication and who can think and respond quickly, succinctly and positively.

5. **Select and Call Back those You Want to Meet:**

   ➤ Since everyone who has called is automatically pre-registered for the event, you are under no obligation to respond personally to every message.

   ➤ However, there will be some people who leave messages who sound particularly promising, and whose participation would help you reach your hiring objectives. Call them first, conduct a Micro-Interview over the phone (see Issue # IV, below) and issue them a personal invitation to come to the event so you can meet them face-to-face.

6. **Comment on using Voicemail for this Purpose:**

   ➤ It's amazing what you can learn over the phone, and how valuable this kind of tool can be in helping you determine which of the respondents you want to pursue – particularly if the position(s) you're looking to fill involve sales, customer service and/or telephone skills. This technique is also a good way to discourage tire-kickers, as it asks them to make an effort up front.

Issue # IV:

How to Interview a Large Number Of Prospective Candidates in a Relatively Short Period of Time (i.e., Pre-Screening a Walk-In Or Conducting Interviews At A Job Fair, Open House Or Discovery Session)

◈ **Your Objectives:**

> ➢ To meet and greet all interested attendees.
> ➢ To select those with whom you want to follow up.

◈ **Conduct a 5-Minute Micro-Interview**

> ➢ A Micro-Interview consists of three steps:

>> 1. Introduction:

>> "Hello, _(prospect's name)_, my name is _____ and I'm the _title_ (here) at _(company)_. As you may know, we _(USP statement)_ and are currently looking to fill a position (some positions) involving _(brief description of key job function)_. While I only have about five minutes to speak with you right now, I'd like to ask you some questions that will help me know how best to follow up with you. . . . OK?"

>> 2. Questions:

>> • "Give me a *brief* summary of your training, and of your work activities over the past 18 months."

- "What brings you the point of making a career move? What's your number one career objective in making such a move?"
- " (prospect's name) , my final question is a little different from what you might expect, and I'd like you to take a few seconds to think about it before giving me your answer. Give me the three adjectives that best describe the way you approach your work."

3. <u>Close/Next Steps</u>:

- <u>If you have zero or marginal interest in following up</u>: "Thanks for your time,   (name) , and for sharing this information with me. Once we've had a chance to review our notes, we'll be in a better position to know the next steps. That should be in about a week. Thanks again."

- <u>If you have some interest in following up</u>: "Thanks for your time,   (name) , and for sharing this information with me. Once we've had a chance to review our notes, we'll be in a better position to know the next steps. That should be in about a week. Why don't you call me next _____ -- I should be in a better position then to tell you where we stand. Thanks again."

- <u>If your interest is strong</u>: "Thanks for your time, _____, and for sharing this information with me with me. Based on what I've heard, I think I'd be interested in exploring things with you further.

What does your schedule look like in the next __(few days, week)__ ? . . . Good -- why don't you call me on _____ so we can set up another meeting? Thanks again."

➤ Comment on the Micro-Interview:

- The Micro-Interview can be expanded very easily from a five-minute process to twenty or even forty minutes, simply through your use of follow-up questions. In fact, easy expandability is one of the inherent dangers of the Micro-Interview – which will require a degree of discipline and control on your part to keep the conversation inside the time brackets you need to enforce.

- Here's a way to implement your Micro-Interviews that will help you keep them under control:

  - Since your main objective when conducting a Micro-Interview is to develop enough information to determine whether you'd like to speak with this individual again later, you are gathering basic facts about a person rather than probing for a deeper understanding.

  - Therefore, during a five-minute Micro-Interview you will be asking "fact" questions, only – i.e., questions that begin with "who," "what," "where" and "when".

  - "How" and "why" questions probe deeper. Save them for another time, *after* you've justified your time investment with the "facts."

When you think of all the resources that are currently available for finding candidates for the positions we need to fill, it seems amazing, somehow, to hear a Hiring Manager say that he or she "cannot find anyone who can do the job." And yet, this is becoming a very common lament, one that we will be hearing even more often as the reverse demographics of the baby boom generation – which were outlined in Chapter One: *Read This Book* – continue to take their toll over the next ten years or so. These negative trends are exacerbated by hiring practices that focus on Hard Skills to the exclusion of Soft Skills, and which reflect too narrow a view of the options and avenues that are open for identifying potential candidates

What can you as a Hiring Manager do to turn this sense of scarcity around for your company? Here are two very strong recommendations:

1. **Lead the way in magnetizing the hiring process for your company.** Take the steps necessary to remove the barriers to hiring that may be in place in your firm, and make sure everyone on your staff understands the critical importance of creating a decisive, inviting hiring environment where everyone who interviews with you ends up wanting to work for your organization. Take the steps necessary to ensure that your team knows how to answer the key question – "Why should I quit my job and go to work for your company?" – in a way that generates positive results. Get the community and the marketplace working for you, and you'll be rewarded with the opportunity to select from the best.

2. **Develop a recruiting plan that draws upon as many sources of potential candidates as possible.** This plan can be as simple as a checklist of types of sources to call for referrals, periodicals to place ads and bulletin boards to post opportunities. Make sure that all of the bases that have been listed here are covered, as well as the additional sources that you develop locally. Approach your sources hierarchically – as demonstrated here – so that you are always taking advantage of prior work, moving from the known to the unknown. Beware of the common definition of the term, "networking" -- which has been grossly devalued through improper usage to mean five phone calls to three friends (usually with no results) – and do some real networking, reaching out to everyone you can think of who is, may be, or may know the person(s) you seek. Make calls to some unusual sources – like AARP, University Department Heads, vocational, professional, ethnic and civic organizations – and ask for referrals to prospective candidates who may fall outside your normal hiring community. And make the personal commitment, whether you are currently hiring or not, to always be on the lookout for the next person you could add to your team.

Hiring Managers who take this approach quickly develop an outlook and attitude that runs directly counter to the idea that good candidates are "scarce." To the contrary, as the referrals and contacts begin to flow in increasing numbers, these Managers find that prospective candidates are everywhere, and that their challenge is to select the best from a very good lot. And while winnowing out the nuggets in the midst of an abundant harvest presents some problems of its own, these Hiring Managers will tell you unanimously that these problems are much, much better than the "scarce" alternative.

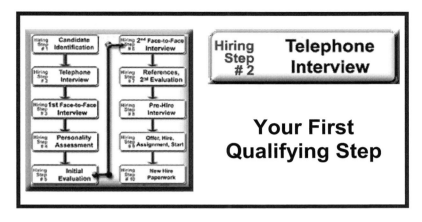

Hiring
Step
2

Telephone
Interview

Your First
Qualifying Step

Except in the case of people with certain physical challenges, using the telephone as a first-level qualifying device is appropriate in almost every situation. It certainly makes sense with candidates for sales, customer service and telemarketing positions, as the telephone will be used as a primary tool in the exercise of their duties. But beyond that, the phone interview is a great way for you as Hiring Manager to *compress time*, and it can . . .

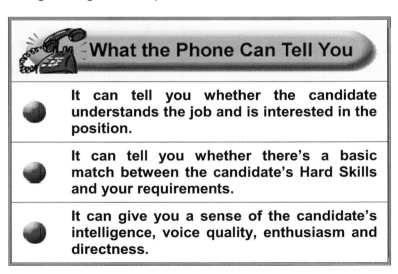

What the Phone Can Tell You

It can tell you whether the candidate understands the job and is interested in the position.

It can tell you whether there's a basic match between the candidate's Hard Skills and your requirements.

It can give you a sense of the candidate's intelligence, voice quality, enthusiasm and directness.

What the Phone Can Tell You

 It can tell you about the candidate's ability to listen.

 It can demonstrate candidate's verbal skills, voice inflection and ability to interact in a conversational manner.

 It can give you some initial information about the candidate's personality style.

In short, a well-executed telephone interview will tell you enough about the candidate to help you determine whether or not to invest the time to meet the candidate face-to-face. And speaking with a series of candidates on the phone over a relatively short period of time can give you a strong feeling about which ones you would like to see first.

These arguments *for* the use of the phone interview as an initial qualifying tool are presented with the following caveat: some personality styles fare better with the phone than others. Using the DISC model, for example, high "D" (Dominance) and "I" (Influence) personalities will generally fare better on phone interviews than high "S" (Steadiness) or high "C" (Compliance) personalities. These differences are heightened when the "S" or "C" candidate is matched up on the phone with a "D" or "I" Hiring Manager, as each personality style is seeking different cues than the person on the other end of the phone is most comfortable giving. Because of these differences, depending on the position(s) for which you are interviewing, it would be a mistake to discount a candidate simply on the basis of his or her phone skills, if the other needed factors were in evidence.

How do you conduct an effective phone interview? Here are some detailed guidelines:

Phone Interview Guidelines

1 Introduce Yourself:

"Hello, _(prospect's name)_ , my name is _____ and I'm the _title_ at _(company)_ . We received your resume from _____" or "I was referred to you by _____. As you may know, we _(USP statement)_ and are currently looking to fill a position involving _(brief description of key job function)_ . Have I reached you at a time when you can speak freely?"

2 Set the Stage:

"_____, my purpose in calling you today is to gather a little more information about your background and objectives, and to answer any questions you might have, to see if we have a match. We should be able to get that done in about 10 minutes."

Phone Interview Guidelines

3 Ask <u>Your</u> <u>Questions</u>:

❖ "I see by your resume that you've done some work with _____. Could you tell me a little more about that experience?" (etc.)

❖ "What brings you to the point of making a job change? . . . Could you develop that a little more for me? . . . What do you see as your ideal next step?"

❖ As a way to give me a handle on how you like to work, what three adjectives would you use to describe the way you approach your job? . . . Why?"

4 Ask <u>For</u> <u>Questions</u>:

❖ "_____, what questions can I answer for you at this time?"

Phone Interview Guidelines

5 Provide Feedback:

◈ "_____, given what we've discussed so far, I think it might be worth our while to get together to explore the possibilities in more depth. How do you feel about that? . . ."

-or-

◈ "_____, given what we've discussed so far, it doesn't seem like we have enough of a match to take things further at this time. Thank you for taking the time to speak with me today."

6 Establish Next Steps:

◈ "Good. What does your schedule look like over the next _____?"

-or-

◈ "_____, I'd like to be able to contact you in the future if our situation changes. And in the meantime, if you do happen to meet someone who has the _____ experience we need right now, I'd really appreciate a call. Thanks again."

If you are unused to using telephone interviews as part of your screening process, it may seem difficult your first time through the process to both gather the information you need *and* make a decision about whether to proceed to the next step. If necessary, of course, you *could* arrange for the prospective candidate to call you back later to establish next steps, or even commit yourself to make a follow up call to him or her. In general, however, this is not a very good idea, for two very good reasons:

1. **It Could Cost You Some Good Prospects**: Your prospective candidate probably does not yet know enough about the opportunity to know for sure whether he or she wants to pursue it. Your delay might seem like a discouraging sign that pushes him or her in a different direction. It's important to remember, here, that all that's stake is an interview, an investment of 20 to 75 minutes at the most. If you have good feelings about a prospective candidate, you are well advised to apply the following rule: "If some doubt, have no doubt." Bring the prospective candidate in and find out what you need to know.

2. **It Might Cause Unacceptable Prospects to Pursue You to the Ends of the Earth**: Sometimes our hesitance has more to do with a desire to avoid giving a prospective candidate negative feedback than it does with our inability to decide about his/her rightness for the position. This is a case where you should apply the following rule: "If there's that much doubt, rule him or her out." Tell him or her "no," now, so as to save time and heartache for both of you.

Your purpose in conducting a telephone interview is to probe for just enough information to decide whether to invite the prospective candidate to become a candidate, i.e., to include him or her in your continuing hiring process. This is a relatively simple decision, and your checklist of criteria need not be very long. In general, you'll be asking yourself the following eight questions, the answers to which should flow naturally out of the phone interview:

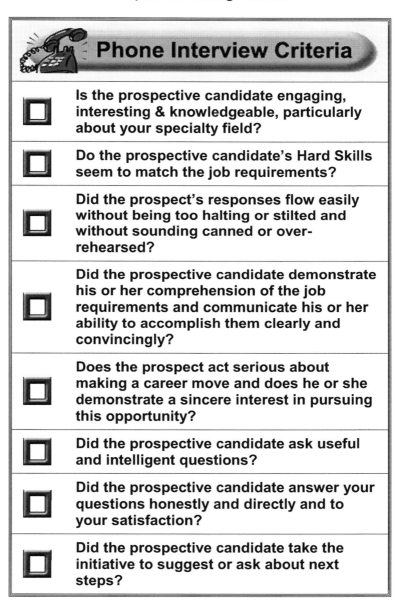

Phone Interview Criteria

☐ Is the prospective candidate engaging, interesting & knowledgeable, particularly about your specialty field?

☐ Do the prospective candidate's Hard Skills seem to match the job requirements?

☐ Did the prospect's responses flow easily without being too halting or stilted and without sounding canned or over-rehearsed?

☐ Did the prospective candidate demonstrate his or her comprehension of the job requirements and communicate his or her ability to accomplish them clearly and convincingly?

☐ Does the prospect act serious about making a career move and does he or she demonstrate a sincere interest in pursuing this opportunity?

☐ Did the prospective candidate ask useful and intelligent questions?

☐ Did the prospective candidate answer your questions honestly and directly and to your satisfaction?

☐ Did the prospective candidate take the initiative to suggest or ask about next steps?

You'll notice that as many of the items on the checklist are "subjective" queries having to do with the nature of the conversation and the rapport you established with the prospective candidate as with his or her "objective" skills and experience. Both types of criteria are important, to be sure, but since the telephone interview is the first hurdle in establishing a working relationship, the phone is a great tool to begin your assessment of a prospective candidate's Soft Skills.

How many of the criteria listed above should a prospective candidate be allowed to "fail" from the list above and still make the cut? Once you've taken into account the personality style issues that relate specifically to the job you are trying to fill (i.e., the job requires a high "C" personality and you are a high "I"), not very many. If the job requirements are highly technical and rely mainly on documentation and written communications, then you might ease up a bit on your assessment of the prospect's verbal skills. And if the job relates to sales and relies heavily on the prospect's persuasive abilities, you might take a somewhat less-than-literal tack when probing his or her specific product knowledge. Yet overall, the prospects you convert into "Candidates" by inviting them to come in to meet you and your staff in person should score well on the eight-point test shown above.

Bottom line? If the phone interview goes well and you feel it's worth your time to meet the prospective candidate in person, invite him or her to participate in the next step. If the prospect flunks your test, be gracious and decline. Used this way, the phone interview is a time management tool that will keep your initial selection step simple and the hiring process moving forward.

Hiring **1st Face-to-Face**
Step
3 **Interview**

Qualifying the Candidate And Selling The Opportunity

The 1st Face-to-Face Interview is the setting where the foundation will be set for everything that follows. Those all-important first impressions will be made by and for all parties. As Hiring Manager, this will be your first chance to explore the Candidate's Hard and Soft Skills in depth, and it will be the Candidate's chance to impress you with his or her abilities and to get his or her initial questions about the job opportunity and the department and company answered.

In order to achieve your goal of hiring right via a hiring process that is both thorough and decisive, your challenge will be to control the conduct of the interview in such a way as to cover all the bases within a relatively short period of time. For the 1st Face-to-Face Interview, that time could be as short as 20 minutes, but in no case should it be more than an hour. It's best to keep this interview to 45 minutes or less.

The key to achieving this goal is preparation for the interview. As stated in Chapter 4 -- *Hiring Blunders We All Have Made*, there are four areas where preparation will pay you dividends:

1. Reviewing the Candidate's resume in light of the job requirements and noting key questions and areas of focus;

2. Adding your list of questions that will help you get at the Candidate's Soft Skills;

3. Writing up some bulleted agenda points on how you'd like the meeting to flow (see next page); and,

4. Refreshing yourself on the preparation work you've done to sell the company, the department and the opportunity to the Candidate.

How should this interview be conducted? The following illustration will give you an idea of what topics to cover, what kinds of questions to ask, and the key items you're looking for during this first interview:

Conducting the 1st Interview

Topic, Questions & Comments, Key Objectives

1. Interview Introduction:

Questions to Ask:

- (After some warm-up) "_____, as you know, our purpose in getting together today is to explore the idea of you coming to work for us as _____ in our _____ department."

- "During our time together today, I'd like for us to cover …

Conducting the 1ˢᵗ Interview

Topic, Questions & Comments, Key Objectives

- "Some questions I have about your work background, skills and experience;
- "An overview of _____ Company and the career opportunities we offer here;
- "Your objectives, work style and why you are considering a change at this time; and,
- "Any questions that you might want to ask me."

- "As I think you know, _____, this is an important hire for us, and the person who is chosen will be meeting with us more than once over the next week or so. For this reason, I'd like to keep this first meeting to forty minutes or less."

Key Objectives:

- To Set The Stage And Tone For The Interview
- To Establish The Interview Agenda
- To Set A Realistic Expectation About Time

2. Background, Experience and Skills:

Note: How you approach this part of the interview will depend greatly on what the Candidate's resume shows you versus your job specifications. But even if the resume indicates the Candidate is a "perfect match" for the position, you'll need to do some probing to find out for sure.

Conducting the 1st Interview

Topic, Questions & Comments, Key Objectives

Questions to Ask:

- "_____, I can see by your resume that you've worked with _____ on several different projects. Could you summarize how these projects have deepened your understanding of _____ and what knowledge level you've achieved because of them?"

-or-

- "_____, according to your resume, you've sold advanced cash management products to commercial customers for three different banks. That's interesting, but I'd like to hear more about the size of the customers you called on, and the typical titles and reporting levels of the people you were working with within those companies. . . . What's been your largest single sale to date? . . . What's your average sale?"

-or-

- "Have you had hands-on experience with _____? . . . Tell me about it."

-or-

- "I see you did your Master's Thesis on _____. How have you used that in your job?"

Conducting the 1ˢᵗ Interview

Topic, Questions & Comments, Key Objectives

Key Objectives:

- To Verify The Candidate's Hard Skills
- To Determine The Depth And Applicability of Those Skills To Your Situation
- To Get a Sense of the Candidate's Ability to Learn and Apply New Hard Skills

3. Company Story:

This is where you "sell" the industry, the company, the department and the career opportunity to the candidate. This part of the interview does not have to take a long time, but is critically important.

- With a little preparation, your sales presentation can be boiled down to three or four items, like:

    - "_____ the _____ industry that we're a part of is currently about $_____ in size in the US and is growing at a rate of ___% per year. That's good news for career security and growth.

    - "As you may already be aware, our company is best known for its
    _____(USP Statement)_____ and is

Conducting the 1st Interview

Topic, Questions & Comments, Key Objectives

__(stats about company stability, growth, size)__ . What may not be as well-known is that we're currently involved in an initiative that will increase our focus on __(relevant product, project, technology or trend)__ , meaning new opportunities for __(career growth, job variety, increased sales, etc.)__ ."

- "Our department is comprised of __#__ professionals. The thing everyone seems to like best about this team is that they _____ ."

- "It's also interesting to note that the job under discussion has a history of being a __(springboard for promotion, training ground, role no one wants to give up, etc.)__ . Over the past _#_ years, for example, _#_ people have _____, generally after doing a good job for about 3 years.

Key Objectives:

- To Cast The Opportunity Being Offered In A Favorable Light

- To Impel Every Candidate To Want And Actively Seek The Job

- If The Selling Points Presented Here Were All Developed Or Adopted In Concert With Your Staff, Then They Will Be Reinforced Throughout The Hiring Process

Conducting the 1ˢᵗ Interview

Topic, Questions & Comments, Key Objectives

4. The Candidate's Questions:

You can often learn as much about a Candidate's attitudes, motivations, personality and character traits by his or her questions as by the answers he or she gives to your questions. If the Candidate does not ask questions on his or her own initiative, open the conversational space by pausing for a moment, then saying:

- "_____, before we proceed any further, I'd like make sure you get your questions answered. What questions do you have of me? ..."

- Make careful note of the Candidate's questions, or of the fact that he or she had none. For help on how to control the amount of time that this part of the interview may take, refer back to the "Interview Control Techniques" presented in Chapter Four -- *Hiring Blunders We All Have Made*, including:

  - Limiting your initial responses to the Candidate's questions to 30 seconds or less, and changing the focus of the conversation if the questioning process begins to drag on too long . . . by,
  - Saying something like, "That's a good question, _____, and the short answer is . . . (sound byte). I'm sure we can develop this further later on, if need be. Now I'd like to focus on something else. Tell me, ... "

Conducting the 1ˢᵗ Interview

Topic, Questions & Comments, Key Objectives

- If the Candidate draws a "blank," when asked about his or her questions, use prompts like these:

  - "What are your questions about the duties and responsibilities?"

    - and -

  - "What would you like to know about the team interface?"

Key Objectives:

- To Get A Perspective On The Candidate's Level Of Interest

- To Determine If The Candidate Has Done His or Her Homework Prior To Coming To The Interview

- To Gauge The Candidate's Comprehension Of The Job Role And Duties

- To Mine The Candidate's Preconceptions, Motivations And Character Traits

- To Give The Candidate Every Opportunity To Get His or Her Questions Answered, Without Spoon-Feeding

To summarize, the 1st Face-to-Face Interview has two major objectives – to assess the Candidate's Hard and Soft Skills versus the requirements of the position, and to enhance the Candidate's interest via selling points about the company, the department and the job. During the process of conducting the interview, other objectives can be accomplished as well, including:

❖ **Completion of the formal company job application (remember what was said in Chapter 5 – *Hiring Blunders We All Have Made*) about *greeting* the experienced Candidate first, prior to asking him or her to complete that form);**

❖ **Administration of the DISC Personality Survey or other personality assessment tool; and,**

❖ **An initial appraisal of whether the Candidate's compensation history and expectations will fit within the pay range of the position being offered.**

❖ **Gathering the Candidate's reference information, including names, contact information and reference source's relationship to the Candidate, so you'll be in a position to either start the referencing process now or to move quickly when it's time to start taking them later. Remember to focus on the Candidate's prior supervisors and to ask the Candidate what he or she thinks they will say about him or her.**

Once these steps are accomplished, you have one more step to go before you're ready complete your initial evaluation of the Candidate. It's a relatively simple step, one that's made that much easier if you have done the preparation in advance.

Scoring and Interpreting the DISC Personality Survey

If the 1st Face-to-Face Interview has gone as planned, you will have made inroads into the Candidate's Soft Skills – i.e., character, attitudes and personality attributes – via some of the questions you've asked during that segment of the process that is dedicated to the "Candidate's Career Objectives and Work Style."

However, as was asserted emphatically in Chapter Two – *We Hire For Skills; Fire for Personality*, and as was explained in some detail in Chapter Five – *Unleashing the Power of Personality*, Soft Skills and personality assessment are less concrete than the Hard Skills, and are thus more difficult to measure.

For these reasons -- and for the additional insights into how best to manage your new employees once you hire them -- formal personality assessors have been recommended as part of your hiring process, and special emphasis has been placed on the DISC Personality Survey. Here's how you can implement the DISC Survey as part of your hiring process:

Implementing the DISC Survey

1	Do DISC Surveys with your staff and create benchmarks for key positions in your company.
2	Ensure that all parties to the Hiring Process know that the DISC Survey is in place as part of your routine.
3	Conduct Telephone and 1st Face-to-Face Interview s as outlined in this Chapter.
4	At the conclusion of the Face-to-face interview, ask each Candidate you're interested in pursuing to take the Assessor (it literally takes 7 – 10 minutes to complete).
5	Administer the DISC Survey on-line. It will be scored on-line and a 22-page report will be made available to you automatically.
6	Evaluate the results, asking four questions (see commentary on next page for details): • Are the Candidate's personal style graphs congruent? • How closely does the Candidate's style graph match the benchmark for that position? • Does the Candidate's style graph show a "corporate hook?" • (If applicable and needed) Is the Candidate's style graph consistent with someone who is flexible and who can adapt to change?

Here's what the four bulleted evaluation criteria mean in step # 6 in the table just above:

➤ **CONGRUENT STYLE GRAPHS:** As detailed in Chapter Five – *Unleashing the Awesome Power of Personality*, the DISC Personality Survey measures two types of behavioral styles for each Candidate, Learned Behavior and Natural Behavior. It's only when a person's style graphs line up for both styles that an individual can perform a job over a long period of time without undue stress. So if the style graphs look something like this . . .

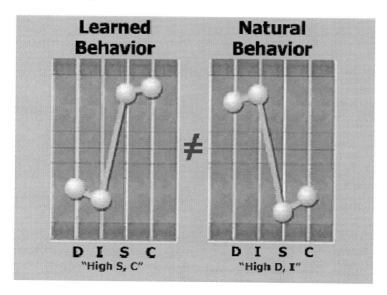

... then they are not similar, not mutually supportive and not congruent. When the style graphs for a Candidate look something like this ...

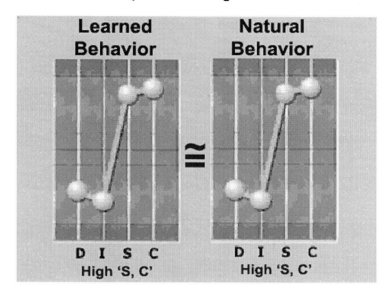

. . . then they are mutually supportive, or congruent. (The graphs do not *have to be* exactly alike – as shown in the illustration above -- to be congruent. They never are in the real world. They just need to be similar enough to be more alike than not.)

➤ **MATCHING THE BENCHMARK** – When your company uses the DISC Survey to map the personality styles of a number of top performers in each critical job function, it can develop style graph shapes – i.e., combinations of Dominance, Influence, Steadiness and Compliance -- that are ideal for each of those job functions. Then your job in evaluating a Candidate's DISC Personality Survey is as simple as comparing his or her style graph to the benchmark. The shapes will either be close or they will not.

➤ **THE CORPORATE HOOK** – Some people have personality styles are so difficult to control that they do not work well in a corporate environment. This can be especially true for hard-driving sales and marketing or entrepreneurial types who continually find themselves at odds with company regulations. One way to counteract this tendency toward willful behavior is to look for salespeople and executives whose personality styles show a corporate hook – i.e., their "S" and "C" scores are below the midline, but their "C" quotient is heading toward a more comfortable, corporate bandwidth. The style graph shown below is a classic example of a strong sales personality style with an acceptable corporate hook:

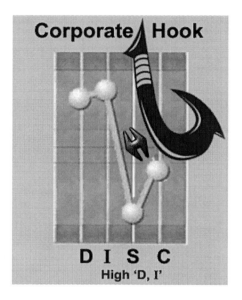

Corporate Hook

D I S C
High 'D, I'

> ➤ **FLEXIBILITY VERSUS RESISTANCE TO CHANGE –** While there is more than one way to ferret out a Candidate's flexibility versus his or her resistance to change, the style graphs can help in this area as well. In general, we know that 'D' personalities like to create change, high "I's" like to stay at the forefront of change (or at least, the appearance of change), an "S's" reflexive impulse is to preserve systems, procedures and traditions in the face of change, and high "C's" will only embrace change if they can see the order within it and find a justification for it in facts and data. It is

therefore reasonable to conclude that high "D, I" personalities will be more likely to see the benefits of change, while the high "S, C" types will be more likely to resist it.

But this last concept must be tempered by what you observe about the Candidate during the interview process. The Candidate who complains during the about reasonable changes to his or her job description and duties in his or her current job, for example, is not only exhibiting poor judgment on the interview, but is also clearly not flexible enough to fare well in a dynamic work environment, no matter what he or she declares to be the case or what the graphic indicators say.

So while it is by no means a perfect divining rod, the DISC Personality Survey can make a great contribution to your hiring process by enabling you to reduce four rather complex concepts to simple, yes/no answers. It can thus be a great help in factoring a Candidate's Soft Skills into your hiring equation, providing useful confirmation for and lending depth and shape to your intuitions about a Candidate's character.

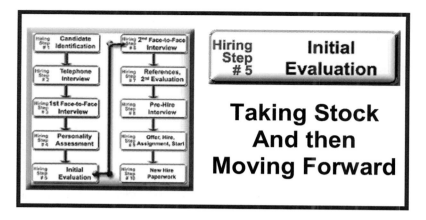

You have now reached the halfway point in your hiring and selection process and are about to start putting the pieces together. Let's assume for the purposes of this discussion that you have three Candidates who have made it through the 1st Face-to-face interview stage. Before making the final commitment to a 2nd Face-to-face interview with any of them, you are best advised to take a moment to review what you've learned so far about each Candidate, to make a "go/no go" decision about proceeding.

Each of the steps that you've gone through so far should have generated impressions and answers to questions that have impelled you to go this far with each Candidate. To confirm that this is actually the case, and to put some force behind your desire to make a balanced decision, ask yourself the following questions about each Candidate based on your experience so far:

Initial Evaluation - Key Questions

1. Candidate's Background:

❑ Does the Candidate have a stable business background and a positive earnings record?

❑ Can he or she cite quantifiable accomplishments?

❑ Does he or she have the requisite skill sets and knowledge of our business or of one that is similar?

2. Interview Performance:

❑ On a scale of 1 – 5, how would you rate his or her phone interview performance?

❑ Was he or she able to demonstrate an ability to make a contribution to the team during the Face-to-face interview?

❑ Was the Candidate honest and direct?

❑ Were his or her questions intelligent and well-thought-out?

❑ Does the Candidate speak and listen well?

Initial Evaluation - Key Questions

3. <u>Comprehension</u> of <u>Job</u> and <u>Business</u>:

❑ Does the Candidate understand the duties and responsibilities of this job?

❑ Has he or she completed this kind of task successfully in the past?

❑ Has he or she had prior successful experience working with our kind of company in our industry?

❑ Has he or she researched our company?

❑ Would much training or coaching be required to get him or her up to speed?

4. <u>DISC</u> <u>Survey</u> <u>Results</u>:

❑ Are the Candidate's personal style graphs congruent?

❑ How closely does the Candidate's style graph match our benchmark for this position?

❑ Does the Candidate's style graph show a "corporate hook?"

❑ Does Candidate seem flexible and open to change?

Initial Evaluation - Key Questions

5. Attitude, Interest and Motivation:

- ❏ Can this Candidate take direction?

- ❏ Does he or she project a positive attitude and/or is he or she easily discouraged?

- ❏ Do his or her career objectives match up with what we're offering?

- ❏ Does the Candidate show initiative and does he or she take an active role in pursuing next steps?

- ❏ Do the Candidate's reasons for leaving make sense, and are they compelling enough to induce him or her to accept a reasonable offer?

- ❏ Would such an offer be in line with what we can pay?

6. Ability to Perform:

- ❏ Does this Candidate seem ready and able to perform the duties of this job?

- ❏ Is he or she excited by the challenge?

- ❏ Will he or she be free to concentrate on this job?

Now that's a long list of questions. You may feel that some of them are not necessary -- and for any given Candidate, some of them probably will not be. Nonetheless, it's a very comprehensive list – which is the point -- and you'll find that most of questions are very easy to answer. You'll notice that unlike the interview questions, which were open-ended, these are couched in terms that encourage "yes/no" answers. That's because the objective here is to make decisions based on the information already at hand, rather than to gather more. There are a lot of questions precisely because this checklist requires you to look at the Candidates through a series of microscopic lenses rather than using a single, wide-angle approach.

When you review each of your Candidates in this manner, you'll be likely to discover one or more of the following:

➢ **You may have formed a very high opinion of a Candidate who is actually a bit weak on some of the factors that are critical to the hire; or,**

➢ **Conversely, you may have developed a lesser opinion of someone else who comes up stronger than you would have thought possible when you measure him or her *vis a vis* the entire checklist; or,**

➢ **Both.**

Whatever you find, you will be better off for having conducted the review. It may cause you to revise your choices as to whom you'll be bringing in for the second round of interviews, but even if it doesn't, the review will arm you with some very specific questions that will make your second round of interviews more precise and to the point.

Once you and the Candidates have committed to the second round, the stakes will be that much higher. Yet your overall objective for the second interview will still be very similar to the first – to gather most of the additional information necessary to make the hiring decision.

To impress this fact on your Candidates, and to test their willingness to verify their claims to competence, this is the time when you should give careful consideration to giving each one you bring back in an assignment that will present you with a practical example what they can do on the job. This could be a sample of the Candidate's work product, if he or she can provide that without violating confidences and proprietary rights, or it could be one of the following:

- **A sample business plan or outline;**
- **A marketing, sales or closing strategy;**
- **An article authored by the Candidate;**
- **A case study;**
- **A sales presentation;**
- **A training presentation;**
- **A proposal;**
- **A set of specifications;**
- **A component design;**
- **A troubleshooting procedure; or,**
- **A sample financial analysis or report.**

This assignment could either be based on a real situation or on a scenario that you create for the Candidate. Whether it's real or made up, the assignment should be something that is relevant enough to the work the Candidate will be doing for you that you will want to review it during the 2nd Face-to-Face Interview and as part of your hiring decision.

With the decisions made, the questions written down, the appointments made and the homework assignments given, you're now ready for that 2nd round of Face-to-Face Interviews.

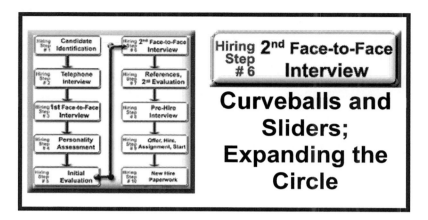

So, OK. You've done your analysis and have decided to invite a Candidate back for a 2nd Face-to-Face Interview. This Candidate has made it into your "semi-finals." Now is the time to expand your circle and put the Candidate to the test.

At this point you need to re-confirm the positive impressions gained on the first interview, to make sure the Candidate is aware of and can handle the negatives as well as the positives of the job, to delve more deeply into the Candidate's Hard Skills, Soft Skills and deficiencies, and to enlist the input of key members of your team.

Here is a list of eight critical checkpoints you'll want the Candidate to navigate successfully if he or she is going to make it through the 2nd Face-to-Face Interview and into the "finals":

Critical Candidate Checkpoints

1 Did your overall impression of the Candidate "hold up" -- i.e., did the Candidate seem at least as strong during the second interview as he or she did during the first?

2 Did your relationship with the Candidate "deepen" – i.e., did the foundation that the two of you laid down during the first interview serve as a platform for progress, or did you feel like you had to "start over"?

3 Did the Candidate respond appropriately to the "negatives" of the job?

4 Was the Candidate straightforward, truthful and non-defensive in his or her responses to your feedback regarding his or her weaknesses – and did he or she either rectify your impressions or put forward a reasonable approach for overcoming them?

5 Was the feedback from your team members acceptable and did it conform to your own "take" on the Candidate?

6 Did the Candidate bring in his or her "homework assignment"? Was it responsive to your original request and acceptable as a piece of work?

7 Did the Candidate continue to show enthusiasm about the job and did he or she push for the next step or offer?

(continued)

Critical Candidate Checkpoints

8 Do you still "like" the Candidate? Can you actually visualize him or her working for you and making a positive contribution to your team?

To a certain extent, the 2nd Face-to-Face Interview is the inverse of the first – in the sense that it is less about selling and more about qualifying and re-confirming. While the tone you set for the interview should be positive, your questioning process should be much more incisive, and your focus should be on the Candidate's staying power. Thus, with the exception of a Hard Skills "depth check" by one or more of your staff members if you feel a "technical interview" is needed, most of your emphasis should be on exploring the Candidate's Soft Skills.

Curveballs and Sliders

Don't be afraid to surprise the Candidate by throwing a few curveballs and sliders into the mix. In order to make the judgments you'll need to make, you may need to push the Candidate off-balance a bit. Your purpose is not to do harm, but rather to get to the truth, to move the Candidate out of his or her "best foot forward" mode so that you can get a glimpse of his or her "true self." The "true self" is the one that that will only come to the fore during times of boredom, unhappiness, frustration, conflict or stress.

Here are five curveballs and sliders that, if used judiciously, can be very instructive in helping you develop a deeper insight into your Candidate's character:

1 The Negative Sell:

❖ The purpose of negative selling is to test the depth to which the Candidate is committed to overcoming the obstacles that the job may put in his or her way.

❖ The negative sell is very straightforward. Just lay out the negatives of the job (every job has them) in a serious manner, slowing down your normal cadence of delivery for emphasis. When you're done, say, "Well, what do you think?," or, "How are you going to handle these problems?"

And then be quiet.

❖ If the Candidate says something like, "I don't know. I'd have to think about that," thus trying to avoid dealing with your question in the here and now, his or her emotional commitment to the job is not that strong.

❖ If he or she says something like, "Do you mind if I take 30 seconds to think through my answer before I respond?," your curveball has thrown him or her a bit off balance but he or she is still in the game. Listen closely to the response. If it's plausible and sincere, then the Candidate has passed your test.

(continued)

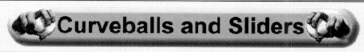

❖ If he or she has ready answers for your question, listen carefully to make sure they don't sound glib or rehearsed. If they don't, and the answers are credible and delivered with conviction, then the Candidate has passed your test with flying colors.

2 The Reverse Sell:

❖ This technique is very much like the Negative Sell, except that your role as questioner is more assertive, and you are asking the Candidate to *sell you* on his or her strategies for untying the knots that go along with accepting and performing the job, rather than trying to sell him or her on how you think he or she ought to address them.

❖ Probing the Candidate regarding the counter offer, which was addressed in some detail in Chapter 4 – *Hiring Blunders We All Have Made*, is a prime example:

❖ Using reverse selling, you would approach the Candidate this way: "_____, I know we've spoken about this before, but I need you tell me again. If we make you a reasonable offer and

you accept, what are you going to do when your current supervisor makes you a counter offer?"

❖ The Candidate is likely to say, "I'll turn it down." If he or she says anything less definitive, you've got trouble.

❖ Assuming the Candidate says he or she will turn it down, respond by asking, "Why would you do that?"

❖ If the Candidate can't give you a convincing answer to your "why" question, you've got trouble.

❖ If the Candidate *does* give you a convincing answer, no matter what it is, challenge it, by saying something like, "Well, what if your supervisor offers you a big raise or a promotion, or both?"

❖ Listen carefully to the tone and cadence as well as the content of the Candidate's response. If it is principled and plausible and is delivered with conviction, then you're probably all right. If it's anything else, you've may have trouble lurking just ahead.

❖ You can use this same kind of Reverse Sell for a range of issues where you need to double-check that the Candidate is really prepared to do what's necessary to take the job and shoulder its responsibilities, should you decide to make him or her an offer.

❖ Other examples would include how he or she is planning to present the opportunity to his or her spouse and family, and how he or she intends to develop any new skills or competencies that are required by the position.

3 The Pause:

❖ The Pause is a technique you can use when you ask a Candidate a tough question, and the answer you get back seems inadequate or less than the entire truth.

❖ With the Pause, you use silence as a way to give the Candidate a chance to expand on his or her initial statement.

❖ Let's say that you have just asked a Candidate about a time gap or discrepancy in his or her resume, and the answer you've received – some swallowed words about "consulting" – is less than satisfying.

❖ You could attack the "consulting" issue head-on. But the problem with this approach is that you are very likely to force the Candidate to dig

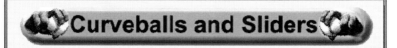

Curveballs and Sliders

his or her heels in without bringing any new information to the fore.

❖ Silence is a much more powerful and effective tool. Just maintain eye contact with the Candidate while saying nothing. Keep it up longer than is comfortable for either one of you.

❖ The Candidate is likely to respond in one of three ways:
  i) He or she will start talking again and will say more, usually getting closer to the truth you need to hear;
  ii) He or she will ask you a question like, "Is something wrong?," or,
  iii) He or she will try to change the subject.

❖ If the Candidate starts talking again, listen carefully. Use follow-up questions to direct the conversation toward a satisfactory answer.

❖ If the Candidate asks you if something is wrong, say, "No . . . it just seemed that you had more you wanted to tell me about this . . ." And then be quiet again.

❖ If the Candidate changes the subject, it's likely there's something that he or she is trying to hide, and you'll have to ask yourself whether it's worthwhile to continue the interview.

Curveballs and Sliders

4 Log Rolling:

◈ Use this technique when you perceive a flaw or problem with some aspect of an otherwise strong Candidate's attitude or ability to do the job, and you want to see if he or she has the humility – and the gumption -- to overcome it. In effect, you take your concern or objection and send it rolling like a log across his or her path, to see how he or she reacts.

◈ The key to your success with this method is that statement of the flaw or problem must be very direct and clear.

◈ For example, you might have occasion to tell a Candidate who has worked in Product Management, and who now wants to make the transition into pure Sales, something like this:

◈ "_____, there is no question that you have the product knowledge to provide our Customers with good support, but both your assessment scores and your prior work history tell me that you may be too analytical and methodical to be able to make impromptu presentations and move quickly to the close in our fast-paced environment."

◈ The only acceptable response to this log you've rolled at the Candidate is a bit of a fight. You want him or her to prove his or her mettle to you by jumping over the log you've rolled and demonstrating that you're mistaken.

❖ If the Candidate asks to see the assessment score or to take some time to think about what you've said, or if he or she says anything approaching, "I guess you're right," then he or she has confirmed your negative suspicions and has flunked your test.

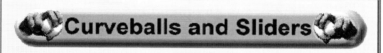

5 The Columbo:

❖ Do you remember Columbo? He was the TV detective played by Peter   Falk who seemed perpetually disorganized   and confused, yet who always managed to end each show with a "zinger" or "gotcha" that resulted in the arrest of a key suspect.

"Gee, I'm a little confused."

❖ The Columbo is a great way to respond to a Candidate when he or she makes a statement that contradicts something that he or she said earlier. The technique is designed to prompt the Candidate to confront the contradiction and clarify or resolve it.

❖ There are four components of an effective "Columbo":

Curveballs and Sliders

(a) <u>Timing</u> – Columbo was a master of timing. Make sure you take timing into account as you implement the steps presented below.

(b) <u>Delayed Reaction</u> -- When the questionable statement is made by the Candidate, pause long enough to imply that you have accepted his or her answer, so that the Candidate relaxes. Make it seem as if you're ready to go on to other topics.

(c) <u>Transitional Phrase</u> – You'll need to use a transitional phrase to bring the conversation back to the topic you want to address. Columbo would have said, "Gee, I'm a little confused . . ." but something like "Wait a minute, I just had another thought . . ." or "Uh, oh, yeah, there's just one more thing I need to clear up . . ." will work just as well.

(d) <u>Follow-up Question</u> – Craft your follow-up question so that it poses the problem you're having with what you've been told without sounding accusatory. Just lay it out there, and ask the Candidate to clear it up.

❖ Here's an example of how you might use the Columbo:

- YOU: "Well, OK, _____, that makes sense." (Pause)

- YOU: "And I guess that brings us to . . . (Pause, Pause)

- YOU: "Oh, wait a minute -- something just occurred to me."

- CANDIDATE: "What's that?"

- YOU: "Well, during our first interview, you told me that the most important thing in making a career move is the opportunity to grow with a company that has a clear vision. And yet you just told me now that you would consider a counter-offer with your current firm for the right money. So which is it: vision and growth, or money?"

It's important when using interviewing techniques like the ones shown above to keep these tools in perspective. You purpose in employing Curveballs and Sliders is not to "trick" your Candidates, but rather to get at the information you need in order to make an informed hiring decision. Of the five, you would probably only use Negative Sell, Reverse Sell and Pause regularly, and you would use the other two, Rolling Logs and Columbo, more sparingly, only when needed.

Think about it this way. If you have to use these techniques with a Candidate too often, that means one of three things:

1. The Candidate is unsure about or feels that he or she is unsuited for the position; or,

2. You are not totally convinced that the Candidate has the requisite Hard Skills or temperament for the job; or,

3. The Candidate has made some important statements that are either self-contradictory or don't sit right with you, and which require a lot of your effort to resolve.

By contrast, you will find that you will use such devices with your best Candidates only on rare occasions. These Candidates will be solid in their Hard and Soft Skills, will demonstrate a sincere readiness to tackle the challenges that accepting and doing the job will pose to them, and will conduct themselves in a way that is consistent and gains positive momentum from interview to interview.

Questions to Ask, Items to Cover

As you move through the 2nd Face-to-Face Interview, you are closing in on the moment when you can pull all of the information together to make your hiring decision. Whereas the events surrounding the interview process previously required scheduling and were only partially in your control, you will now have the opportunity to move quickly and decisively. As was pointed out in Chapter Four – *Hiring Blunders We All Have Made* – moving quickly and decisively is critically important at this stage, as Candidate expectations will be sky-high and time kills all deals.

Two additional considerations will thus be added to your interviewing task:

1. **To ensure that all of the necessary bases are covered; and,**

2. **To clear the way for fast action once a decision is made to make an offer.**

You can use the following pointers to pull them all within your grasp:

Pointers for the Second Interview

 A. <u>Confirm</u> the <u>Candidate's</u> <u>Hard</u> <u>Skills</u>:
- ◈ Use follow-up questions from the first interview.
- ◈ Gather additional input on the Candidate from your staff.

 B. Have <u>Key</u> <u>Staff</u> <u>Members</u> <u>Interview</u> the <u>Candidate</u>:
- ◈ Select participating staff.
- ◈ Brief on the first interview.
- ◈ Instruct on the additional information you need to learn.
- ◈ Coach on questions to ask and questioning technique, if needed.

 C. <u>Confirm</u> and <u>Explore</u> the <u>Candidate's</u> <u>Soft</u> <u>Skills</u>:
- ◈ Ask "Why", "How" and "What If" questions.
- ◈ Use Curveballs and Sliders, as needed.
- ◈ Determine what the Candidate feels strongly about professionally and why.
- ◈ Pose real-life work challenges from your environment and ask the Candidate how he or she would handle them (and why).
- ◈ Review the Candidate's homework assignment, testing him or her a bit by challenging his or her assumptions. Use the assignment as a way to learn more about how he or she thinks.

Pointers for the Second Interview

D. Probe the Candidate's Readiness to Go to Work for You:

❖ Say then ask, "As you probably know, _____, if you were to go to work here, your starting salary would be no more than $_____. Is that amount acceptable to you?"

❖ Ask, "Knowing what you know now, _____, if we were to make you that kind of offer, would you accept?"

❖ Say then ask, "I know we've covered this before, _____, but I want us both to be prepared. What's going to happen when you go in to your boss to resign? . . . (etc.)"

E. Present and Address the Negatives of the Job:

❖ Introduce the negatives like this: "_____, the last time we talked, we spent some time going over the reasons why people like working here at _____. As I remember our conversation, you indicated that of the six or seven things we went over, _____, _____ and _____ were the most important to you at this stage in your career."

"As you look at that conversation now, do those reasons still hold true? . . ." (If the priorities have changed, find out why and nail down the current list.)

Pointers for the Second Interview

"Ok, good – I'm glad we clarified that. As I'm sure you know, no job or company is perfect, and we're no exception. In our case, there are __(#)__ things that I think you might find troubling. They are:

- _____;
- _____;
- _____; and,
- _____."

❖ Now close by asking, "How are you going to handle those issues when they come up while you're working here? . . .," then listening closely to the Candidate's response.

 F. Gather and Hypothesize References:

❖ If you haven't already done so, ask the Candidate for the need for the names and contact information of past supervisors and co-workers. Tie down names, titles, phone numbers, email addresses and timeframes of the relationships.

❖ For those reference contacts that are most current and relevant, ask the Candidate, "_____, what do you think _(former supervisor)_ is going to say about you when I contact him or her?" Listen carefully.

❖ Then ask, "_____,"what three adjectives would he use to describe you? . . . Why those particular words?"

Pointers for the Second Interview

G. Ask for and Answer the Candidate's Questions:

❖ If the Candidate hasn't asserted his or her questions to this point in the second interview, make sure they get addressed now. Say and ask:

"_____, we're both getting to the point we're going to need to make some decisions. We've been asking you a lot of questions today, but I'm sure you have some for us as well. What are your questions? . . . What else? . . . What else? . . ."

❖ Since the evaluation phase of the interviewing process is drawing to an end, you want to achieve three objectives with regarding the Candidate's questions:

- To prompt the Candidate to put all of his or her questions on the table;

- To answer those questions to the Candidate's satisfaction; or,

- To establish a distinct process and a short timeframe by which the Candidate's questions will get answered.

❖ As the 2nd Face-to-Face Interview draws to an end, it's time for closure on both the questions and the answers. To accomplish this, use "tie-down" phrases

Pointers for the Second Interview

to get agreement that the answers are complete: "_____, that answers your question about _____, doesn't it?"

❖ Then do a wrap-up of all of the questions and answers by asking, "_____, I think that takes care of the entire list, doesn't it?" . . . (If yes) "Good. I'm glad."

 H. <u>Summarize</u> the <u>Interview</u> with the <u>Candidate</u>:

❖ Because so many things have to happen before they are complete, second interviews often have a way of trailing off with no real conclusion. A formal application is filled out or a meeting takes place with Human Resources, and then the Candidate leaves.

❖ This is a mistake. A more effective approach is to have the Candidate come back to see you for a summary at the end of the day's activities.

❖ The summary can be brief, but it includes a vital probe. Say it like this:

"_____, I want to thank you for coming in and spending time with us today. I know we ran you around a bit, but it was a very productive time, and you've given us the information we need to make our decision. I trust we've done the same for you."

"Before you go, _____, I'd like to ask you just one more question. Leaving the

Pointers for the Second Interview

issue of money aside, on a scale of 1 – 10, 10 being the highest, how would you rate your current level of interest in the position?"

If the Candidate says he or she is an "8," ask, "Money aside, what would it take to move your '8' score to a '9.5'? . . ."

(You may be able to use this information to create a "sweetener" for the offer.)

Then close: "_____ we'll be in a position to get back to you in about _____ days. In the meantime, please call me if I can help you in any way. I'll talk with you soon."

(continued)

Pointers for the Second Interview

I. <u>Make</u> <u>Sure</u> <u>all</u> <u>Pre-Hire</u> <u>Paperwork</u> &
<u>Procedures</u> <u>Are</u> <u>Handled</u>:

❖ Even though you haven't made the decision
to hire this Candidate yet, you'll still want to
take care of all paperwork that is required
prior to the hire, so that it doesn't hang you
up once you decide to make an offer. While
not all items shown will apply to every
situation, here's a checklist of the kinds of
paperwork and procedures you may need to
have in place so you can expedite the offer
once the decision is made:

❑ Clean Resume Original

❑ Completed Employment Application

❑ Meeting or Interview with Human
Resources

❑ Summary of Company Benefits
Information for the Candidate

❑ Government Clearance Documents

❑ DISC Personality Survey or other
Personality Assessment

❖ Most of the items listed above can be
handled during the 2nd Face-to-Face
Interview, if they haven't been completed
before. Planning is the key to getting it all
done.

Once you have covered the items shown above and have
completed the 2nd Face-to-Face Interview, you are ready
to evaluate whether to make this Candidate an offer. That's
Step #7 in the Hiring Process.

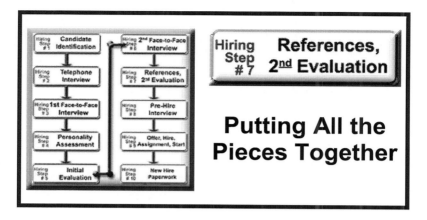

Putting All the Pieces Together

If you have met with more than one Candidate who has made it through the 2nd Face-to-Face Interview successfully, you probably have a pretty good idea by now of who you want to hire. If so, you'll be facing the temptation to get on with it, to make a decision based on your gut instinct, alone -- to make an offer and complete the hire. If only one Candidate has made it this far through the process, you may feel driven by a sense of scarcity or urgency to make an offer to that one, whether or not he or she is really up to your standards.

Either way, you could be making a mistake, as was emphasized in Chapter Four – *Hiring Blunders We All Have Made*. While you are now further along in the hiring process than you were at the 1st Face-to-Face Interview stage and have more information at your disposal, there are three powerful dynamics at work that could pull you in the wrong direction:

1. **Recency – We tend to be drawn to the last Candidate with whom we have had a positive interview simply because we can still remember the details of the conversation.**

2. **Similarity – We tend to like the Candidate best who is the most similar to us in temperament and personality, even if those characteristics are at**

odds with the fundamental requirements of the position we're trying to fill.

3. **Convenience and Simplicity** – Hiring right takes real work, and the process can be taxing. The Candidate we have before us may become more attractive than he or she really should be simply because hiring him or her is easier than going through the complexity and paperwork involved in gathering all the feedback and completing the references.

There are two actions that must be completed before you'll be in a position to make an offer decision. First, if they haven't already been done, complete the reference checks, using the guidelines presented in Hiring Blunder # 5 in Chapter 4 (obviously, from the point of view of timing, it would have been best if you had begun the referencing process once you had committed to bringing the Candidate back for a 2nd Face-to-Face Interview). As you are completing that process, conduct a top-to-bottom evaluation of each Candidate, using a rating sheet like the one shown on the next two pages.

You'll have to use your imagination a bit, here – putting a single column of the Prospective Employee Rating on each of two facing pages was the only way to show its features here in readable form. The actual Rating Sheet you would use would be self-contained on an 8 ½ X 11 sheet of paper:

PROSPECTIVE EMPL

Evaluation Benchmarks	Ratings

1 Background of Candidate:
A   Approp. Bkgd. & Education
B   Measurable Achievements
C   Successful ___ Experience
D   Useful Process Knowledge
E   Progressive Track Record

Subtotal #1 ➜   (25)

2 Performance on Interviews:
A   Positive Phone Interview
B   Enthusiastic about Opp'y
C   Handled Job Negatives Well
D   Positive Feedback: Staff
E   Positive Feedback: Mgt.

Subtotal #2 ➜   (25)

3 Comprehension of Job & Duties:
A   Quick to Pick Up Concepts
B   Likes Primary Job Activity
C   Grasps Spec'l Require'ts
D   Embraces Work Standards
E   Assumes Responsibility

Subtotal #3 ➜   (25)

4 DISC Assessment Scores:
A   Has Corporate Hook
B   Match to Preferred Style
C   Overall Benchmark Score
D   Sample Interview Questions

(X2)
Subtotal #4 Times Two ➜   (40)

OYEE RATING SHEET

Evaluation Benchmarks	Ratings

5 Reference Check Results:
- A Initiative, Work Ethic, Team
- B Accomplishments Verified
- C Customer, Staff Interface
- D Would Rehire (No Hesitation)
- E Recommended for this Job

Subtotal #5 ➜ (25)

6 Homework Assignment Results:
- A Implemented Instructions
- B Completed Assignment
- C Made Clear Presentation
- D Competent Defense of Ideas
- E Made a Useful Contribution

(X2)

Subtotal #6 Times Two ➜ (50)

7 Overall Assessment:
- A Shows Initiative, Pursuit
- B **Can Handle Learning Curve**
- C "Fits" with Culture, Team
- D Manageability Rating
- E Will Accept Offer

(X2)

Subtotal #7 Times Two ➜ (50)

Final Scoring: Tally of Subtotals

#1 + # 2 +   #3   +   #4   (115)

=

#5   +   #6   +   #7   (125)   + (↓)

=

(240)   = (↓)

GRAND TOTAL ➜   (KO < 161)

You may remember that Hiring Blunder # 3 in Chapter Four was "Making Hiring Decisions Too Much by Gut and Not Enough by Systems and Metrics." This Prospective Employee Rating Sheet is your antidote for that particular brand of poison. While the sheet might seem a bit complex at first glance, a closer look will reveal that it follows the basic sequence of the Hiring Process itself, and that it asks a series of questions that are relatively easy to answer.

Most of the questions ask you to make judgments that are at least partially subjective. That's OK – as hiring itself is at best a subjective art. The key to this evaluation is not that it reaches some lofty, objective standard by which your Candidates can be calibrated, but rather that it challenges you to make a number of subjective assessments, each looking at the Candidate from a slightly different perspective. In the example shown above, 34 factors are considered as part of the evaluation. It's the sum total of all of these observations -- taken together -- that gives you the basis for evaluating your Candidates and comparing them to each other.

You record your assessments by selecting a rating number for each factor presented. Your rating number choices are 0, 1, 3 and 5, only, which are defined in the Rating Key that is positioned at the lower left-hand corner of the sheet you would normally use (but is not included in the illustration on the previous pages):

Rating Key

5 = Excellent Match to Criterion
3 = Good Match to Criterion
1 = Partial Match to Criterion
0 = No Information or No Match to Criterion

These rating number options -- 0, 1, 3 and 5 -- are used to force a "spread" in the results, as the evaluation tool is only useful if the numeric scores come out differently enough between Candidates to help you clearly distinguish between the leaders and the also-rans.

In addition to leaders and also-rans, the Employee Rating Sheet also identifies losers.   The following Scoring Yardstick is positioned in the lower right-hand corner of the sheet (not shown on the previous two pages:

```
┌─────────────────────────────────────────────┐
│            Scoring Yardstick                 │
│             240   =  Perfect                 │
│      216  to  239  =  Excellent              │
│      181  to  215  =  Acceptable             │
│      161  to  180  =  Marginal               │
│        0  to  160  =  Unacceptable           │
└─────────────────────────────────────────────┘
```

This Yardstick sets a standard by which you can determine Candidates who, by your own measure, do not meet a standard that you feel to be acceptable for hire by your organization.   The standard set in the example is reasonable one – with a minimum acceptable score of 181, it is about equivalent to the requirement that a college student maintain a "70" average to stay in school, or the rule that a fledgling pilot must get at least 70 percent of the questions right on his or her written test to qualify for a private pilot's license.

This Scoring Yardstick will help you do two things:

1. **If you have only one Candidate who has made this far, it will tell you whether you should make an offer or look for someone better.**

2. **If you have a number of strong contenders, it will help you rank those who pass muster and disqualify the rest.**

Developing the scores is important, but what is even more important is what the Final Evaluation process does for your thinking. It is often said that the toughest discipline in Management is taking the time to review our activities properly, and that our most important Management "products" are good decisions. Even if your Final Evaluation accomplishes no more in a given hiring situation than to confirm your intuitions, by doing so it will strengthen your actions.

You are therefore strongly advised NOT to skip this crucial Final Evaluation step in the Hiring Process, and to use an evaluation tool like the Employee Rating Sheet shown above to conduct your evaluation in a consistent and systematic manner. Here are some guidelines to help you along your way:

Evaluation Guidelines
Don't worry if you are a high scorer or a low scorer. Just be consistent.
If you're coming up with a lot of zero's because of insufficient information – stop the evaluation and go get the information.
If your team is participating in the evaluation, have each member fill out his or her own Prospective Employee Rating Sheet and then compare.
Low Candidate scores are sometimes negotiable. If the Candidate is strong in most areas, bring him or her back in, use the Log Rolling technique and see what happens.

Evaluation Guidelines

 If the numbers don't add up, the Candidate probably doesn't, either. Take your lumps and move on.

 Modify the criteria as needed, but place your trust in the system. The best Candidates WILL receive the highest scores.

Your evaluation is complete, you have factored in the Candidates' Hard Skills and Soft Skills, you've supplemented and validated your intuitions with metrics, and you now know who you want to hire.

It's time to implement the strategies that will bring that person on board.

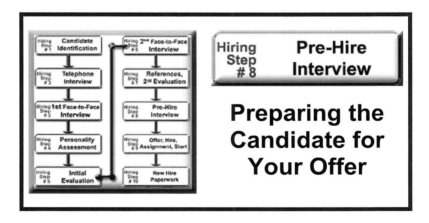

It would be great if making an offer and getting an acceptance were as simple to do as to say, but consider the following statistics: in good employment markets and in bad, over one-third of all offers are turned down, and about one-fifth of those who do accept an offer never show up for work at the new job. And as Candidates become scarcer and jobs become more plentiful as the economy heats up, those statistics only get worse.

As was pointed out in *Hiring Blunder #10 -- Getting Surprised at Offer Time* -- in Chapter Four, there are lots of forces at play in the employment marketplace that give aid and comfort to a Candidate's natural fear of change at that crucial moment when an offer is put on the table.

Because of these forces, it is usually NOT a good idea to make an offer directly after the 2nd Face-to-Face Interview. A much better strategy is to engage your "finalist" in 3rd Face-to-Face Interview, with five objectives in mind:

➤ **To reinforce the positives of working together;**

➤ **To address any outstanding questions or issues about the job;**

➤ **To revisit the Candidate's position on resigning and turning down the inevitable counter-offer one more time;**

➤ **To hypothesize (or pre-test) the offer; and,**

➤ **To earn approval for your selection.**

The "Approval" aspect of the Pre-Hire Interview is more important than it might seem at first glance. Even if your company is very small, your hiring process will be best served if it proceeds according to the three phases depicted in the diagram on the facing page:

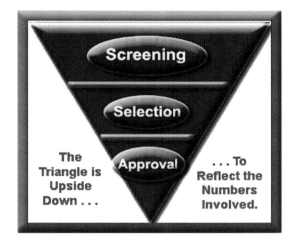

Here's how these three phases mesh with our Hiring Process model:

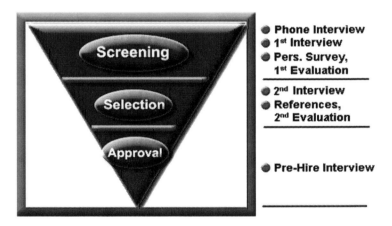

Approval by whom? It depends on your position in the company. But even if you're Chairman of the Board charged with the task of hiring a new President, you report to the other Board members, and a Hiring Committee should be constituted to approve your selection. Under most other circumstances, the person serving in the approval role will be your direct supervisor or boss -- the person to whom you report.

If your hiring process does not currently include an Approval phase, it would be a good idea to create one. While there are many reasons why this is an essential and useful business practice, here are three that focus squarely on hiring:

1. **It provides a strong justification for why a Candidate should come back for the 3rd Interview;**

2. **It frees you up as Hiring Manager to focus on the operational issues while someone else keeps his or her eye on the 'bigger picture'; and,**

3. **It positions you properly for Candidate requests and negotiations, by giving you the ability to temper instantaneous commitments via an "appeal to a higher authority."**

A surprising number of Hiring Managers -- and an even greater percentage of Candidates -- have a tendency to underplay the importance of the Approval part of the Pre-Hire Interview. Hiring Managers sometimes describe this final meeting as a "rubber stamp" interview, even to Candidates – which is a mistake. And Candidates make an even more grievous error when they believe that description.

True, a Candidate may have successfully navigated an arduous maze to get to this point, but that doesn't mean that he or she has "got it made." While very few "boss's bosses" relish the idea of overriding the selections their managers have made, most will do it, if necessary. After all, making tough decisions is a large part of how they got to their current positions within the company. And the last thing most of them need to see in an interview is a Candidate whose ego has been inflated to such an extent that it appears to be a full order of magnitude greater than his or her potential contribution.

Preparation and Setup

Here are four rules of thumb for setting the proper expectations and tone for a successful Pre-Hire interview with your finalist:

 Setting Up the Pre-Hire Interview

1. Describing the Purpose of the Meeting:

❖ Think "medium gravity." -- i.e., let the Candidate know it is a serious meeting without making it sound scary.

❖ Tell the Candidate what's going to happen:
- Meet with my boss.
- Talk about the job.
- Ask and answer any 'final' questions.

 ### 2. Coaching the Candidate for the Meeting With Your Boss:

❖ While you are, in effect, the Candidate's advocate for this meeting, don't volunteer information about your boss unless asked.

❖ Note: This is a bit of a test -- a resourceful Candidate who wants to be well prepared WILL ask.

❖ When asked, be very balanced in what you present to the Candidate about your boss. Be careful NOT to say anything *about* him or her that you wouldn't say *to* him or her.

Setting Up the Pre-Hire Interview

3. Meeting Pacing & Sequence:

❖ Establishing control over timing, sequence and pacing is very important to the Pre-Hire Interview. Here are the rules of thumb:

❖ The entire meeting, from the time the Candidate arrives until he or she leaves, should not take more than 1 ½ hours.

❖ Here's how the process should work. Note both the order and timing of what is presented:

(a) The Candidate meets with you to be briefed, first. 5 - 10 minutes, max.

(b) The Candidate meets with your boss. Keep that meeting to 30 minutes or less, if possible, even if you have to knock on the door and interrupt to bring it to a close.

(c) The Candidate meets with anyone else who is absolutely necessary, only. For example, the Candidate might need to meet with someone in Human Resources, to discuss the transition to the new benefits package. 10 - 15 minutes, max.

(d) The Candidate meets with you to debrief and get any final questions answered.

Setting Up the Pre-Hire Interview

 ### 4. Your Role, Style and Tone:

❖ Your role in this session will be a mixture of four things:
- ■ Advocate
- ■ Coach
- ■ Re-qualifier
- ■ De-Briefer and Hypothesizer

❖ Your personal style needs to achieve a balance between serious and informal.

❖ Resist the temptation to set too chummy a tone with the Candidate. Maintain your professional distance. He or she has not come to work for you yet, and too close is not compatible with the signal you want to transmit.

 ### 5. Debriefing the Candidate:

❖ You'll want to know how the Candidate feels it went with your boss. Cover:
- ■ How it went generally.
- ■ Specifically what was discussed.
- ■ Where the Candidate felt he or she did well and where he or she could have done better.
- ■ How the boss left it with the Candidate.

Setting Up the Pre-Hire Interview

 ### 6. Pre-Testing the Candidate:

❖ You'll want to know:
- If all of the Candidate's questions have been answered satisfactorily.
- If the Candidate will accept the position, if offered.
- When the Candidate could start work.

The list of "thumb-rules" shown just above gives you a yardstick not only for the issues you'll be addressing, but also for the roles you'll be playing in the Pre-Hire Interview. As such, it's a strong start on a plan for the meeting itself. In order to complete your planning for the Pre-Hire Interview, you will need to add the following two activities to the list shown above:

1. **Preparing your boss for the meeting.** Assuming he or she has not already met the Candidate, your would be arming your boss with the following five pieces of information:

   (a) A copy of the resume and a summary of the Candidate's "paper" qualifications.

   (b) A capsule of your observations of the Candidate during the interview process.

   (c) Your justification for why you feel this is the best Candidate for the job, including a thumbnail comparison with other Candidates you've seen.

   (d) Your best estimate of the dollar requirements to hire this Candidate. Note: it's better to aim a little high, here, than to have to come back later for more.

(e) Specific topics you'd like him or her to focus on where you could use more information or confirmation of your impressions.

2. <u>Prepare yourself for the meeting</u>. While you will probably not be making a formal offer at the meeting, you *will* be pre-testing one. So in addition to assembling any notes on questions, Curveballs or Sliders that you have left over for this Candidate, you will also need to generate the following information and decisions prior to the Pre-Hire Interview:

(a) The dollar amount you are prepared to offer;

(b) The details and approximate value of the fringe benefits;

(c) Anecdotes and selling points regarding the intangible benefits of working for your department and company;

(d) Hiring sweeteners, if any; and,

(e) Start date provisions, training dates, etc.

(f) Basic data on required agreements – employment contract, confidentiality and intellectual properties agreement, non-compete agreement, etc., if applicable.

A Different Kind of World

In a perfect world, having done all of this planning and preparation, you would be rewarded as follows:

In a Perfect World:

◈ Your Boss would be thrilled with the first Candidate you presented to him or her; and,

◈ Your offer and the Candidate's acceptance would be an instantaneous slam-dunk; and,

◈ The Candidate's spouse or significant other would call you as soon as he or she heard the news and thank you profusely; and,

◈ The resignation and transition would go off without a hitch; and,

◈ The Candidate's former employer would call you in the spirit of good sportsmanship, would thank you for giving the Candidate such a stellar career opportunity, and would ask you what he or she could do to help with the Candidate's transition; and,

◈ If relocation were involved, it would proceed at a brisk pace, with no hassles, worries or trauma;

- AND -

◈ The Candidate would complete his or her first work assignment for the new job *before* he or she actually reported to work.

Unfortunately, that's a world we inhabit only on very rare occasions, and then mainly when we're asleep. During our waking hours, we need to employ a strategy that will effectively handle hiring situations for a world where things don't always go the way we'd like.

For this reason, NOTHING has been said about MAKING the offer yet. What has been discussed, instead, has been about PRE-TESTING it – i.e., making a specific, though hypothetical, offer one more time before actually extending a real one. There are two very good reasons why this is the correct strategy at this point in the Hiring Process:

1. **It's a much better tactic to hold off on the offer until after the Candidate has accepted it (more on this later); and,**

2. **Most Candidates make their career decisions at home, involving spouse and family or significant other, and sometimes extended family members and mentors. Any acceptances given during the Pre-Hire Interview will be held up for scrutiny and review once the Candidate gets there, anyway. And those reviews sometimes result in reversals.**

By pre-testing the offer with the Candidate this one last time, you have one more opportunity to smoke out his or her true feelings and hidden concerns BEFORE putting him or her in a position where he or she has to say "Yes" or "No" to the offer. You may recall that a great deal of emphasis was placed on this way of handling the offer in *Hiring Blunder #10 -- Getting Surprised at Offer Time* -- in Chapter Four, as a way to avoid last-minute reversals.

Your final session with the Candidate during the Pre-Hire Interview will also be the first time you will mention a specific offer amount. This way, the Candidate will get an idea of what you're prepared to offer should the final decision go his or her way, and he or she will thus be leaving the meeting with some substance.

Managing Expectations

The worst thing you could possibly do when pre-testing an offer to a Candidate is to propose an amount that is greater than what you can actually deliver. The only way that one won't backfire on you almost immediately is if the Candidate has no other option than to take the offer you make. Even then, your actions will leave a bad taste with the Candidate that will linger and eventually affect his or her attitude and job performance. Offer pre-testing is clearly a time to exercise some caution.

For this reason, your best bet is to hypothesize an offer that is LESS than you know that you can deliver. This way, if the Candidate says "Yes," your options are open, including:

➢ Leaving the actual offer the same as you stated it in your hypothesis; or,

➢ Sweetening the actual offer by the total amount you originally had in mind; or,

➢ Sweetening the actual offer to a position somewhere in the middle, thus providing the Candidate with a positive surprise and saving some money.

And if the Candidate says, "No," this approach gives you some negotiating room to sweeten the offer without busting your budget.

How to Say It

Your final objective in conducting the Pre-Hire Interview is to get the Candidate to say "Yes" or "No" to your hypothetical offer, preferably yes. "Maybe" or "I'll think it over" is the answer you want to avoid at any cost, as it's a waste of time. When a Candidate says "I want to think it over," it could be a sign of emotional procrastination, as described in *Hiring Blunder #10 -- Getting Surprised at*

Offer Time -- in Chapter Four, with some possibility that a happy solution can be reached, or it could be a sign that the Candidate is planning to use your offer as a bidding chip, either with his or her own company or with another. It's worth a little of your time to have a go at converting this "Maybe" into a "Yes" or "No," but only if you are in control of the conversation.

Here are some sample questions and statements that will help you navigate these swirling waters with success:

Pre-Testing the Offer

1 **Conduct the Debrief:**

Debrief the Candidate on his or her meeting with your Boss, first. Cover:

- What was said
- The Candidate's concerns
- How it was left

2 **Address any Questions:**

Address any questions you or the Candidate may have, including questions about:

- Skills, job roles, duties and responsibilities
- Fringe benefits
- Work content issues
- Policies and procedures
- Technology
- First project

Pre-Testing the Offer

3 Transition to the Offer Pre-Test:

Say something like:

- "You know, _____, I think we could work together well, and that you could make an important contribution here. I sense that you feel the same way – am I right?"

4 Pre-Test the Offer:

(Assuming a positive response):

- _____, as you know, we've reached the stage where it's just about time to take the next step. All I need to do is have a conversation with ___(your Boss)___, and do a little paperwork and then we'll be ready to make our decision.

- Just to make sure still on track, if I were to make you an offer of _$ (precise dollar amount)_, would you accept? . . . (Silence until the Candidate responds.)

- If "I'd have to think about it," see # 5, below.

- If YES: "That's good to hear, _____. Assuming I got you a written confirmation of that offer right away, how soon could you resign and report for work? (etc.)"

- If NO: "Gee, _____, I'm a little surprised. Why not? (Silence until the

Pre-Testing the Offer

Candidate responds.)

- If the Candidate responds to your "Why not?" question with something reasonable, pause to consider it, and then say: "Well, _____, that's a bit of a stretch, but maybe we could do something like this: _____. Would that be acceptable to you?" (Pause)

- If YES: "OK, _____. Then if I offer you __$_____ plus the additional _____ we just discussed, you will accept, is that correct?"

5 The Candidate Wants to "Think Over" the Potential Offer:

If the Candidate responds to your Offer Pre-Test by saying, "I'd have to think it over," say:"

- Good, _____, I'm glad you want to give it real consideration. Tell me, what is it about working for __co.__ that you want to think over, is it the _____?

- Now go through a list of positives and potential negatives about the

  job until the Candidate identifies the one that is a concern. Then probe the issue until you determine whether or not it can be fixed.

- If the Candidate's problem CAN'T BE FIXED, tell the Candidate it can't, thank him or her, and terminate the meeting.

- If the problem CAN BE FIXED, fix it, then

Pre-Testing the Offer

ask the Candidate to confirm that it's fixed. Once he or she has confirmed it to your satisfaction, go back to your original Offer Pre-Test question, and modify it to encompass the fix:
"_____, if we offer you _____, including _____, you will accept, is that right?" (etc.)

As you are going through the steps outlined above, be careful to do two things.

First, Watch and listen to the Candidate very carefully. His or her body language, eyes, voice tone, and pauses will tell you at least as much as his or her words. Be on the lookout for qualifiers and whisker words which detract from the power of his or her responses and thus convey a less-than-genuine response.

Second, if the Candidate expresses a concern, slow down and take the time to understand it before you answer it. Use questions and phrases like, "Could you develop that for me?" and "Why is that a high priority for you?" and "So what I hear you saying is _____ . . ." to identify and nail the concern down before answering it.

These two actions should create the following results:

1. **By paying close attention to the Candidate's words, voice tone and body language, you'll receive clear signals about when to bear down and when to let up in pursuing a commitment from the Candidate.**

2. **By taking the time to delve into the Candidate's concerns during this high-stakes conversation,**

you'll convey a level of caring that will contribute to the possibility of a positive result.

When the Offer Pre-Test has been completed to your satisfaction, your position with this Candidate has reached and enhanced state. You have a sturdy concept of what the Candidate will do when the offer is made, and the offer target has been defined. The Candidate's interest in the opportunity has been rekindled and is rapidly reaching its peak. All that is left is to take the final steps – steps that should be taken within the next 48 hours.

For now, it's best to stay in character, resisting the urge to make the offer until you've completed the Approval phase and can call the Candidate with good news. Say words like these as you bring the Pre-Hire Interview to its conclusion:

"_____, I think we've had a very good day. We've had some very productive meetings, and we've accomplished a great deal.

"As you know, we we're just about ready to make our final decision, and I think you know that you are very much in the running. I'm looking forward to the possibility of working with you and I sense that you are, too.

"So as not to string things along, I fully expect to be back to you, one way or another, within the next two days."

Hiring Step #9 — Offer, Hire, Assignment, Start

Achieving and Solidifying The Acceptance

The good work you've done during the Pre-Hire Interview is now about to pay off. The Candidate has already made the commitment to accept your offer. This frees up at least some of your attention to work on solidifying, or cementing, the acceptance as well as achieving it. Because of the work you've already done, both activities – the acceptance and the cement -- should require only a little time.

First, the acceptance. These five "Do's and Don'ts of Offer Acceptance" will help you get it done:

Do's & Don'ts of Offer Acceptance

DO: get back to the Candidate quickly – within 48 hours. Call in the evening or on the weekend if necessary.

DON'T: take the Candidate for granted. Begin the conversation by reconfirming your prior meeting: "When we talked last _____, you said _____. Is that still correct?"

DO: add a sweetener if possible. Say, "Well, I've got good news. Not only do you have the job, but I was able to add an extra _____ to your _____. . . . Are you ready to accept and go to work?"

DON'T: get shocked or flummoxed if the Candidate waffles or tries to negotiate for more in this imperfect world. Use the Columbo or Log Rolling technique to hold your ground and turn the Candidate around.

DO: congratulate the Candidate and confirm the start date. Let him or her know that a confirming letter will be sent immediately.

Now, the cement. From the moment the Candidate accepts your offer, he or she is no longer a Candidate; he or she's your New Hire. From that moment on, you want him or her to be mentally reporting to you. To the extent that you can achieve this state, then your chances of losing him or her to a counter offer during resignation will be greatly reduced.

Here are seven steps you can take to reinforce the strength of the growing bond between you:

Strengthening the Bond

1 Craft the letter so that it confirms the New Hire's acceptance of the offer, rather than putting the offer forward again. Include all of the particulars of salary, title, start date, interim contact. Make sure it goes out immediately.

Strengthening the Bond

2	Send the Candidate a Congratulations or Welcome card – add a hand-written note.
3	Give the Candidate a small project to do during the interim period – something that requires an opinion rather than a lot of work or research, something that you know will spark the Candidate's interest.
4	Find out when your New Hire plans to resign. Ask him or her to call you as soon as that meeting is over.
5	In case your New Hire is "shown the door" on the day that he or she resigns, establish the start date on an "on or before" basis. Make sure your New Hire knows that he or she is welcome to start work early, at his or her option.
6	Maintain informal communication with the New Hire throughout the period between the acceptance and when he or she reports to work. No heavy agenda – just "checking in to see how you're doing."
7	Assign two additional people the task of making contact with the New Hire during that same time frame from within your organization: ❖ Someone who can answer the Candidate's administrative questions; and, ❖ Someone at the same level as the New Hire from within your department or team with whom he or she can identify.

These simple steps will mean a great deal to your New Hire, and will increase the odds that he or she will report to work as planned. Once you have taken them, Congratulations are in order for you, too.

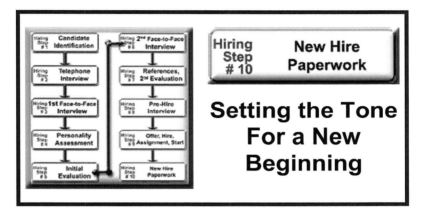

Hiring Step # 10 — New Hire Paperwork

Setting the Tone For a New Beginning

We're almost there. It's now time for the New Hire to report for work. Are we ready? Will he or she feel welcome? Do we have a plan in place to shepherd him or her through those critical first twenty business days? Do we know what to do with him or her on day one?

These may seem like trivialities, but they have an immense impact on the person you bring on board, and thus have a valid place in the Hiring Process. It is beyond the scope of this book to address new employee orientation and indoctrination in great detail. However, the following New Hire Checklist can provide you with a constructive starting point for organizing the task:

New Hire Checklist

☐ New <u>Hire</u> <u>Paperwork</u>:
- ❑ Application Forms
- ❑ I-9 Forms, Employee ID
- ❑ W-4 Forms
- ❑ State Tax Forms
- ❑ Employee Benefits Forms
- ❑ Employee Manual & Briefing
- ❑ EEO & Risk Management Forms
- ❑ _____

☐ New <u>Hire</u> <u>Training</u>:
- ❑ Safety, OSHA & Hazmat Training
- ❑ Software & Computer Training
- ❑ Operations Training
- ❑ Equipment Training & Orientation
- ❑ On-Line Training
- ❑ 20-day Training Plan
- ❑ Training Manual(s)
- ❑ _____

☐ New <u>Hire</u> <u>Welcome</u>:
- ❑ Welcome Sign in Lobby 1st Day/Week
- ❑ Introductions to Staff
- ❑ Team Meeting
- ❑ Newsletter Article
- ❑ _____

New Hire Checklist

New Hire Equipment & Facilities:
- ☐ Desk & Office / Cubicle Setup
- ☐ Computer & Password Setup
- ☐ Supplies & Supply Access
- ☐ Key Access to Building
- ☐ Key Access to Lavatories
- ☐ Email Setup
- ☐ Network & Database Access
- ☐ Internet Access & Policy
- ☐ Parking Accessibility
- ☐ File Cabinets
- ☐ _____

New Hire Business Supplies:
- ☐ Business Cards
- ☐ Brochures & Mailers
- ☐ Phone & Business Directories
- ☐ Stationery
- ☐ Pens, Paper, Desk Accessories
- ☐ _____

New Hire Work Assignments:
- ☐ First Project: _____
- ☐ Second Project: _____
- ☐ Assigned To: _____
- ☐ Committee Work: _____
- ☐ Primary Task: _____
- ☐ Other Duties: _____
- ☐ _____

New Hire Checklist

☐ ## New Hire Objectives:

☐ **First Month;** _____
☐ **First 90 Days:** _____
☐ **First 180 Days:** _____
☐ **First Year:** _____

No matter what measures you take, the first month will be stressful for your New Hire. Yet the best antidote to stress is a plan. Use a checklist like the one shown above to develop a working plan that allows you to anticipate your New Hire's needs and keep him or her focused on the important tasks until he or she finds some bearings and begins to make his or her own way.

We have now completed our journey through the Hiring and Selection process in Chapter Six – *Hiring Winners*, and have tackled a large number topics along the way. The following view of the Hiring Process Flow Chart can serve as a reminder of the path we've taken.

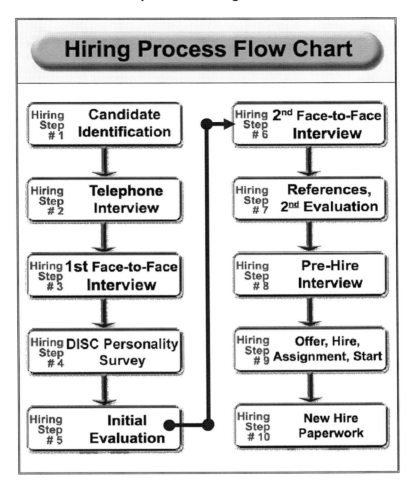

Chapter Take-Aways

Item	Idea, Issue or Action Item	Done / Noted
1	Use multiple sources for identifying prospective Candidates, but prioritize them.	☐
2	Set up a voice mail phone screen system for Candidates where sales or customer service skills are key.	☐
3	Integrate the DISC Personality Survey into the hiring and selection process as a supplement.	☐
4		☐
5		☐
6		☐
7		☐

Note: The purpose of this "Take-Away" page is to encourage you to summarize the key points of the materials you've read in this Chapter. To get the process started, I have listed three items that I feel are important, but this list is not exhaustive.

Take this opportunity to inventory what you've learned and crystallize what you want to implement before moving on.

Chapter Seven

Your Company's Real Wealth

O ne of the most striking implications of our economy's shift in emphasis from manufacturing to services has been the impact of that shift on the source of corporate wealth. Over the past forty years, knowledge has replaced production capacity and access to raw materials as the key element in capital formation. According to business guru Tom Peters, this transformation became apparent and irreversible when the value of Microsoft eclipsed General Motors on the stock market. At that moment it became clear to business persons world wide that wealth had become synonymous with knowledge.

A lot has happened since Peters first made that statement a decade-or-so ago, but the fundamentals are still in place. Now -- with the bursting of the Dot-Com bubble and the ravages of 9/11/01 etched into our psyches -- we may not be quite as starry-eyed as we once were about the virtual future. But it is still valid that knowledge is the key to modern wealth, and that the key to your company's wealth is the knowledge of the people you employ.

True, there are gargantuan quantities of information captured, documented and stored in computers, networks, files, manuals, procedures, protocols, patents and intellectual properties in the possession of many companies. However, this accumulation shrinks to insignificance when compared with the amount of critical information that the people who work for us carry around in their heads – the comparison is simply no contest. For the most part, it is our people who use and apply the information available to them who create the services our companies perform. And in applying that information and providing those services, our employees create the knowledge that is the basis for wealth.

Ask any competent financial planner, and he or she will tell you that wealth is built brick by brick. Except for those very rare instances of overnight millionaires that are the stuff of television series and serve, mainly, as recipes for the misguided, wealth is the product of *gradual and consistent accumulation*. Get-rich-quick schemes don't work, and dazzling new product ideas lose their luster in the Information Age with astonishing rapidity. The only sure way to build wealth for your company is through the day-to-day work of the people who provide your web of products and services.

Why this dissertation on the fundamentals of modern business success? To underscore the significance of the point just made. Your people and the knowledge they accumulate are the real wealth of your company. If you want to build that wealth, you need to create the conditions whereby that knowledge can undergo that "gradual and consistent accumulation," that the financial planners advocate.

In Chapter Three – *The Turnover Treadmill*, dominant emphasis was placed on the high cost of turnover – an annual cost in the $ trillions that currently approaches the amount the US economy spends on health care. Additional focus was placed on what to do when an employee leaves, and on some basic precepts for retaining employees. Here we'll take that process one step further. Drawing on principles already presented in this book, we'll explore eight ideas that can help you stabilize your organization, so that "gradual and consistent accumulation" of knowledge and wealth can occur.

Different is Different, So Players Can Be Winners

In any organization, Managers have a tendency to categorize their employees into three different groups: Winners, Players and Losers. This tendency is a natural one, arising out of the impulse to favor those whose contributions are most dramatic, and to cull out those whose offerings are barely worth the effort. But it's also a mistake – not so much because of what it does to the winners and losers, but because it makes the ones who are caught in the middle – i.e., the Players – fade away into the Land of Invisible People.

All you have to do to convince yourself of the importance of avoiding practices that are discouraging to *any* of your employees is to take another look at the turnover statistics presented in Chapter Three – *The Turnover Treadmill*, and to review what was said in Chapter One – *Read this Book!* about the demographically-based employee shortages that are projected over the next ten years. It's very clear. Given those numbers, any employee who is worth keeping has value, is an asset who must be preserved. You can make a strong start by working to create an atmosphere within your team where all who contribute are Winners. Here are five actions that will help you do that:

Reclaiming Your 'Players'

1 Learn more about each the four DISC personality styles – D for <u>D</u>ominance, I for <u>I</u>nfluence, S for <u>S</u>teady and C for <u>C</u>ompliance. There's enough material in Chapter Five – *Unleashing the Power of Personality*, to give you a strong start on this. Concentrate on those three personality styles that are *least* like your own, so you can truly come to appreciate their unique contributions.

2 Now make some notes about what the consequences would be if you did NOT have the resources represented by all four personality styles at your disposal. For example, you could ask yourself who would:

> ➤ Make the tough decisions
> ➤ Unify and lead teams
> ➤ Document and systematize the company's best practices
> ➤ Tackle the company's administrative details

Reclaiming Your 'Players'

3	**Conduct this same exercise with your staff. Have each team member take the DISC Personality Survey, and then discuss the differences that naturally emerge with the group.**
4	**Because you will have done the homework on knowing how each personality style makes an essential contribution, you will have the insights you need to keep the meeting positive and mutually-supportive.**
5	**Take the ideas and attitudes generated at the staff meeting and apply them to the workplace in general. Let your staff members know that's what you intend to do.**

Bottom line? When you and your staff truly understand the importance of different personality styles, your "Players" can be "Winners," too. Having been reclaimed from the Land of the Invisible, they will be much more likely to stick around and continue their good work.

Train to Retain
Or
Replace and Re-Train

Have you ever needed a mental fill-up, a break from the routine to get some novel ideas, an opportunity to learn something different, a chance to deepen your grasp, enhance your understanding, upgrade your skills or improve your performance? Every one of your staff members needs those kinds of breaks as well. It's a natural impulse – a yearning for that periodic breath of fresh air that allows them to stay interested in their day-to-day tasks.

Honoring this impulse of your employees to increase their knowledge and understanding through various kinds of training can generate benefits that far outweigh the costs. All it takes is a little planning, some ongoing research and a proactive approach to the kinds of activities you'll approve. Here are just a few of the training activities you can institute that can help you enrich the lives -- and amplify the loyalty -- of your staff:

(facing page)

Training to Retain

 Make participation in training a part of every employee's job description.

 To keep training costs in line, aim for a mixture of the following:

- Company-sponsored events
- Informal, internal training provided by you and your staff
- Low-cost outside seminars on generic topics (like negotiating skills)
- Participation in higher-cost training as a reward for exceeding goals
- Teleconference training
- Free training provided by vendors
- In-house study groups
- Cross-departmental briefings
- Cross-training on complementary skills (i.e., Sale and Customer Service)
- Outside speakers

 Ask each person who participates in an outside training event to come back prepared to share something with the group, thus amplifying the impact of the event.

 Build a short (5-10 minute) skill-building component into the agenda of your regular staff meetings. Rotate presentation responsibilities among your staff.

 Provide copies of a motivational book (like Covey's *Seven Habits for Highly Effective People*) to all staff members and lead a seminar on its key points.

Training to Retain

●	Play a sales or safety video and critique it as a group.
●	Add participation in training and willingness to learn as criteria to your employee performance reviews.
●	Conduct, or get someone else to conduct, a presentation skills workshop for all interested staff members.
●	Explore companies that provide on-line computer skills training. Make the training available to your staff and their family members for free or at cost.
●	Offer first-level supervisory training to those in your group who are looking to move up. Make it an eligibility requirement for promotion.

The list of examples could go on and on. The point is that by encouraging your staff to "sharpen the saw," as Stephen Covey says, you stand to reap dual rewards:

1. **You'll get more highly skilled employees; and,**

2. **They'll be less likely to leave the fold.**

Both rewards add to your company's wealth. The alternative, which is to lose key employees and then be required to replace them and train those replacements from scratch, is simply not acceptable.

Fostering Teamwork That Works

The word "team" is overused these days – we hear it so often, in fact, that it has begun to lose its punch. While most Hiring Managers would agree that it takes more than just a group of people to make a team, few can really put their finger on what welds one grouping of people into a real team, while another assortment continues to stumble along as an ungainly gaggle of folks.

Why bring this up in the context of preventing employee turnover and building company wealth? Because as was discussed in Chapter Five -- *Unleashing the Power of Personality*, Hiring Managers who build effective teams create groups whose collective power is greater than the sum of its individual members. That phenomenon is called synergy. Synergetic teams are internal magnets: for their individual members, the experience of being part of such a team is riveting and satisfying beyond normal standards of comparison. It's an experience that engenders a bond and a level of loyalty that is very difficult to give up. So one, very important, wealth-building aspect of great teams is that they usually manage to find ways to stay together.

How do you know if the group you're building is becoming such a team? Use this five-point checklist to calibrate your sights:

When Is It Really a Team?

☐	It's really a team when the group takes initiative and assumes responsibility for its actions.
☐	It's really a team when the camaraderie is obvious and a high level of interaction occurs among the group's members.
☐	It's really a team when the group actively pursues additional opportunities to do its work (i.e., wants to take on new challenges).
☐	It's really a team when its pace of accomplishment accelerates over time.
☐	It's really a team when the group remains focused on its goals and on the needs of its customers.

The checklist above describes the ways a synergetic team behaves; but what can you as a Hiring Manager do to bring that kind of behavior about? Many experts believe that great teams are sparked into being by the need for high performance – that they emerge and rise to the occasion – and that only elevated goals or a shared sense of clear and present danger will inspire people to bring out their best. Others believe that the leader's long-term vision is the key. Others argue that it is the people, or their training and development, or their day-to-day management, that makes the difference.

While opinions differ on what to emphasize, all of the elements mentioned play a part. Here are five areas where the opinions all converge:

Building High-Performance Teams

 Know -- And Communicate -- Where You're Going:
1. Long-term vision
2. Mid-term goals

 Ensure That The People You Select Have What It Takes:
1. Hard Skills
2. Soft Skills
3. Desire for Excellence

 Develop Your Team Members And Give Them The Tools They Need:
1. Training
2. Encouragement
3. Coaching

 Help Your Team Members Stay On Track:
1. Define Measurable Goals
2. Provide Honest Info & Feedback
3. Remove Roadblocks
4. Implant a Sense of Progress

Remember this. There is very little in life that is more satisfying than pursuing your goals and reaching or surpassing them with the help of a great team. Weld your employees into synergetic teams and sustain them there, and very few will ever want to leave.

Becoming a Guerilla Inspector

It's a time-honored catch-phrase – "People *respect* what you *inspect*." Its relevance to stabilizing companies and building their wealth speaks volumes. And here's an interesting corollary: "People respect most what they *don't expect* you to inspect." More than a simple play on words, this statement expresses a baseline principle of modern methods for enforcing performance standards.

Performance standards have value to your organization only to the extent that they are clearly stated, frequently inspected and evenly enforced. Inspections must be frequent and consistent. They must also be a combination of those that are formal and those that are not, those that are scheduled and those that are unexpected and unannounced. The purpose of formal inspections is to raise the standard to its highest possible level. Spit and polish, ten-hut!, everyone putting on their best. The purpose of informal inspections is to make the standards operational, so they work at ground level, on an every-day basis, for the people who have to live with them.

The best way to conduct informal inspections is by getting closer to your team. This means getting involved enough in selected details of their work, and spending enough time in their work areas, so that it's no big deal when you look over someone's shoulder or join in on an impromptu conversation. When your employees are comfortable having you around, and when your involvement in their day-to-day activity seems natural, THEN you'll be able to look beyond the spit and polish and see what's really going on.

But by getting this close to your staff, does it mean that you've "gone over" to their side? Absolutely not. As a true guerilla inspector, you'll always have your mission clearly in mind. Besides, you've got your boss to keep you straight if you ever start to lose perspective.

The benefit of the guerilla approach to inspection is the depth, accuracy and timeliness of the information you'll be able to gather. You'll identify small divergences from standards long before they ripen into problems or fester into crises. You'll be able to enact modest, pro-active, practical adjustments that will make immediate sense to your employees. By doing so, you will achieve group buy-in and keep your team on track.

As a result of this approach, your team members will respect and believe in the standards you enforce. And this, in turn, will increase their sense of security, of the fairness and reliability of the Management process. They'll consequently feel more comfortable staying the course.

Using the "Sandwich Method" for Constructive Feedback

Here's an old saw that we as Hiring Managers should never forget: "Chastise in private; praise in public."

As Hiring Managers who work hard to get close to our people, it's sometimes easy to lose sight of the enormity of the power we wield with our words. Even when they are being irascible and rude with us, our employees live or die by every word we say to them, and they feel that we should stay above the fray in responding to them no matter how they behave. Despite the fact that this often feels to us like a double standard, they're right. Part of our job as Hiring Managers is to understand and moderate the impact of our words by choosing and using them with care.

When we have occasion to give an employee negative feedback, we are challenged to package that feedback in a way that can be heard. After all, our objective is behavior change, not personal demolition. A straightforward way to accomplish that, called the "Sandwich Method," is presented below:

Using the Sandwich Method

 ### 1. Positive Feedback, First

"Sally, I appreciate the very strong and righteous stand you have taken regarding our code of ethics. It's clear to me that you've taken it to heart."

Using the Sandwich Method

 ### 2. Negative Feedback, Second

"However, when you criticize someone personally for their ethics in a staff meeting, you're clearly stepping out of line. I'm going to have to insist that you apologize publicly to _____ and that you promise me that that kind of behavior will never happen again."

 ### 3. Positive Feedback, Last

"Like you, I am very concerned about the standards. When it comes to doing things the right way, you're one of the best people we have. Because you set such a positive example, I'd like to ask you to . . ."

Using a technique like the Sandwich Method is important, for these reasons:

1. The Hiring Manager who can give negative feedback successfully gains an employee's respect.

2. Respect is the basis of trust.

3. Trust is the glue that holds our organizations together.

Implementing Informal Reviews

One of the more haunting themes to come out of exit interviews and turnover follow up studies is the lament of many former employees that they never really knew where they stood while working at their former companies. Almost to a person, these former employees wished in retrospect that they could have had more time with their supervisors talking about how they were doing and what they could be doing to improve. From what they said in the follow up studies, many of these lost employees came to believe that had those conversations taken place, they would *not* have felt compelled to leave their companies.

What these folks are telling us is that their Managers were not giving them the performance reviews they needed to stay anchored. Lacking that information, they felt as if they had been cast adrift, and they responded by eventually floating away.

Let's admit it. Performance reviews are tough. They take a lot of preparation time, the canned corporate formats are often difficult to apply to specific individuals and situations, and they have a way of being weighed down by expectations about bonuses or salary increases that throw a kink into the conversations. Accordingly, many Hiring Managers tend to procrastinate on reviews, putting them off until an hour or so before the annual Holiday Party, speaking with the employee in generalities about his or her performance, and then pushing through a standard salary increase that has more to do with what everyone else is getting than with how that particular individual is performing.

If this scenario hits a nerve, welcome to the club. Too many of us are guilty as charged.

Is there a way to transform performance reviews from negatives into positives? Absolutely. But you have to do two things:

1. **Conduct a more informal type of review, more often; and,**

2. **Make it clear up front that these Informal Reviews are not about money.**

What makes Informal Reviews different is the fact that the money is off the table, the stakes are lower, and conversation is more leisurely and specific. Your function in the session is more as a coach than a judge. And the review spotlights the individual, his or her strengths and weaknesses, and specific actions that he or she can take to improve, rather than emphasizing that person's degree of conformance to an abstract, top-down standard.

Here's an example of an evaluation tool you can use to conduct such a review:

Interim Assessment

Employee Name & Title: Rene Browne

Part I: Basic Qualifying Characteristics

Qualifying Characteristic	Pre-Set Weight	Grade: 1-10	Evidence of Characteristic, Comments
1. Effective Communicator	10	8	Does a great job with clients.
2. Knack for Needed Skills	10	7	Has gone on sales calls with very positive results.
3. Positive Role Model	10	9	Does the business the right way, most of the time.
4. Accountable to Firm's Goals	10	8	Needs an occasional reminder, but is mostly OK.
5. Shares Info, Bus. Leads, Credit	10	5	Needs real work here, because of prior background.
6. Writing & Numbers Skills	10	8	Great with numbers; writing skills need improvement.
7. Can Handle Change	10	7	Doesn't like it much, but deals with it like a pro.
8. Mastery of Systems & Proced.	10	9	Knows our system by heart. Implements it well.
9. Computer, Internet Skills	10	8	No basic problems, but could be faster with Word.
10. Demonstrated Leadership Ability	10	7	Does an acceptable job. Gets flustered in meetings.
11. Production/Job Track Record	10	8	Solid, consistent producer.
12. DISC Survey	10	9	Scores are highly consistent with next job role.
Grading: Total	10	X 93	= 930 / 1200 = 78 % (Min: 75%) ☑ OK ☐ Redirect

Completed by: _Clarence Middleton_   Date: _5/23/05_

The images shown here and on the next page are small -- the normal format is two sides of an 8 ½ X 11 sheet of paper. As you can see, the Interim Assessment is comprised of a two-part form – the first part of which is shown above, with the second part appearing on the next page:

Interim Assessment

Part II: Enhancing Attributes & Compatibility

Enhancing Attribute	Grade: 1-5	Evidence of Attribute, Comments
1. Able to Learn	5	*Maybe almost to a fault.*
2. #'s-Oriented	4	*Knows what they are; sometimes forgets their meaning.*
3. Proactive	3	*A little too passive & reactive. Needs work.*
4. Organized	5	*Good time manager; superbly organized.*
5. Outgoing	4	*To the point where she might do better in pure sales.*
6. Desires Next Step	4	*Has often mentioned a desire to move to the next step.*
7. Team-Oriented	3	*Inconsistent — needs some work in this area.*
8. Style-Flexible	4	*Showed great flex dealing with Martha Zanic.*
9. Confident	4	*Reasonably so — especially about how to sell.*
10. Creative	2	*Definitely needs work, here. Gets it done by tenacity.*
11. Goal-Oriented	3	*Tends to focus on process more than objective.*
12. Focused	5	*Great concentration — tis that with goals &....*
13. Tough	3	*A little too accommodating, but then I'm mean.*
14. Completes Tasks	4	*Almost always if instructed.*
15. Emotionally Stable	4	*Almost always 'up.' Occasionally gets rattled.*
16. Confidence Level	5	*Never afraid to try something new– i.e., Jarvis.*
17. Energy Level	4	*Slight tendency to lose energy toward the end of the day.*
18. Work Ethic	4	*Medium strong; some fatigue factor.*

Scoring:

Total Grade: **70** ÷ # items graded **18** ÷ **5** = **78** % | Minimum Score: 75%

Areas Needing Development: *#13 - Toughness. Assignments needed for each of them.*
Needs work on #3 - Proaction, #7 - Team, #10 - Creativity, #11 Goal Orientation,

Completed by: *Clarence Middleton* Date: *5/23/05*

The most important thing to know about the Interim Assessment is that the number and content of the criteria used are totally under your control. This is a bottom-up format that you can tailor to suit your needs. The scoring system is set up so that it will render a percentage score regardless of the number of items under consideration. In the models shown above, the Assessment forms are benchmarked against a minimum required score of 75%, but you can change that minimum as well.

The Interim Assessment is set up in two parts to reflect the two kinds of skills and attributes you'll be evaluating. Part I, which is labeled "Basic Qualifying Characteristics," focuses for the most part on Hard Skills, while Part II, labeled, "Enhancing Attributes and Compatibility," deals mainly with Soft Skills.

Your purpose in using a tool like an Interim Assessor is to give you a systematic foundation for conducting a review conversation. There are two reasons why so many criteria are listed:

1. **Like the Prospective Employee Rating Sheet presented in Chapter Six, the Interim Assessment is designed to prompt you to look at your employee through the many perspectives of lots of little lenses; and,**

2. **With so many options to choose from, you are bound to come up with a number of attributes you can praise about the employee to add counter-balance to the areas where the employee needs some work.**

In addition to what it can do help you build an agenda for an effective review conversation, one of the most important features of the Interim Assessor is how it prompts you to summarize the Informal Review and identify follow-up steps. On the bottom of the second page of the Assessment is a section entitled, "Areas Needing Development." Here are the notations that our sample manager made:

Areas Needing Development:	➤ Needs to work on:
	   #3 - Pro-action
	   #7 - Team
	   #10 - Creativity
	   #11 - Goal Orientation
	   #13 - Toughness
	➤ Assignments needed for each of these items.

The "Areas Needing Development" section of the Interim Assessment serves as your basis for determining next steps. It encourages you to assign specific projects to your employee that will challenge him or her to stretch his or her capabilities in very specific ways. If a promotion is in the offing, it defines the steps the employee must take to earn it.

Informal Reviews should be scheduled quarterly for most employees, with the exception of the quarter when your company conducts its annual salary reviews.

By implementing Informal Reviews, you will be tackling one of the most dangerous turnover issues head-on. Because of your actions, your employees will know where they stand, and what they must do to improve. You'll stop their drifting and set their anchors firmly back in place.

Reselling the Mission By Revisiting Your USP

If you have developed a Unique Selling Proposition (or USP) for your company or department as recommended in Chapter Six – *Hiring Winners*, you should dust it off and revise it every six months or so – not by yourself, but working with the members of your staff. You would do this with three objectives in mind:

1. **To make sure it accurately reflects any changes to your company's offerings that have occurred during the interim period;**

2. **To refresh and re-energize your USP now that you and your group have had the opportunity to use it for a while; and,**

3. **To give your staff members an opportunity – as they focus on a document that is designed to be used as a selling tool that represents your department and company -- to resell themselves on the value of working for you as well.**

This is an exercise that is best done with a light touch and a splash of levity, perhaps as an ice-breaker at an all-day planning session or as a way to end a morning staff meeting with the aid of some sodas and pizza. Good USP's are a form of poetry, and are best undertaken when the mood is appropriate for brainstorming and the group's creative impulses are at a peak. But don't let the buoyant tone of the session fool you. Retooling your USP is serious business, and the session can have a subtle, profound and positive impact on your group.

Hiring Right is the most effective wealth-building strategy of all. It's also **Your Most Important Job**. See the materials in Chapters Two through Six, above, for details.

Chapter Take-Aways

Item	Idea, Issue or Action Item	Done / Noted
1	Implement a training program, including skill-building sessions at staff meetings and cross-training briefings.	☐
2	Make more guerilla inspections – show up in the back more unannounced, at unusual hours.	☐
3	Implement Informal Reviews and the Interim Assessment form. Get a copy in word and do the revisions	☐
4		☐
5		☐
6		☐
7		☐

Note: The purpose of this "Take-Away" page is to encourage you to summarize the key points of the materials you've read in this Chapter. To get the process started, I have listed three items that I feel are important, but this list is not exhaustive.

Take this opportunity to inventory what you've learned and crystallize what you want to implement before moving on.

Chapter Eight

The Proof Is In the Doing

I began this book by claiming that the topics we'd be tackling are critically important to you as a Hiring Manager and to the future of your company. Hopefully, I've verified that claim to your satisfaction. In addition, I promised that in the course of presenting this material, I would keep the theorizing to a minimum, avoid the use of jargon whenever possible, and provide proven, practical, doable steps to help you implement its key concepts. That's what all the tips, pointers, checklists, tables and primers have been about. Having created the book, I would be highly gratified to hear that something offered here struck such a chord with you that it motivated you to take action.

For that's what it's really all about, isn't it? Training is wonderful, seminars are great, and books are fine, but until we take action and use the information to enhance our business practices, it's all just conversation. The final confirmation – and the only verification that will have real meaning for you – is what you try, what you do, and what succeeds for you. To paraphrase a very old saying, the Proof is in the Doing.

There are only two things left for me to do to help you make a transition into the "doing" phase. The first is to provide you with a summary -- headlines and highlights, only -- of what has been offered here. The second is to recommend some initial actions to get things going.

Chapter Summary and Recommendations

Chapter One –
Read this Book!

Synopsis: **Chapter One** sets the foundation for the book, by spotlighting current practices, trends and changes affecting our hiring practices and the people we hire. It speaks in general terms about the three big issues that will change the landscape of North American business in the next ten years: recruiting, hiring and retention.

Key Point: Long-term demographic trends indicate that there will be 10 million fewer skilled people than skilled jobs in the US by the year 2010. This means that fierce competition for scarce workers is on the way, which will make it much more difficult for companies to hire new employees and retain their existing staff.

Recommendation: Give this problem the serious attention it deserves. Even if the projected shortages are overstated, we are moving rapidly toward an era when companies that are not proactive about their employee recruiting, hiring and retention practices will lose their ability to compete.

Chapter Two –
We Hire for Skills, Fire for Personality

Synopsis: **Chapter Two** demonstrates that for most companies in North America, there is a tremendous imbalance between the reasons why we hire people and the reasons why we fire them. It points out that our current hiring practices are so out of kilter in their overemphasis on Hard Skills over Soft Skills, or Experience over Personality, that they have a negative effect on company operations and contribute significantly to turnover.

Key Points: The chapter draws two important conclusions:

1. **We must find a way to correct the imbalance between Hard and Soft skills by focusing more on personality factors and character attributes when we hire; and,**

2. **Correcting the problem requires redesign of the hiring process, rather than piecemeal fixes.**

Recommendation: Make the needed changes to your company's hiring process, using the information provided in Chapters Four, Five and Six of this book as your roadmap.

Chapter Three –
The Turnover Treadmill

Synopsis: In **Chapter Three**, the cost of voluntary turnover in the US is calculated at almost two trillion dollars per year, which is three times the US defense budget and almost as much as we spend annually on health care. When all of the factors are taken into account, it costs a company about THREE TIMES SALARY to replace each key employee it loses. Given the current annual rates for voluntary turnover, the average company replaces its entire core staff every five years.

Key Points: These turnover numbers are staggering, and must be addressed. The Chapter explores the following elements, using data derived from turnover studies and staffing industry sources:

1. **Five factors that cause employees to leave;**
2. **Six questions to ask when turnover occurs;**
3. **How Hiring Right sets the foundation for reducing turnover;**
4. **New employee motivation patterns that must be embraced; and,**
5. **Characteristics of top hires -- the kinds of employees who are *least* likely to leave.**

The Chapter then presents a set of pointers on conducting exit interviews, included a punch list of topics you'd want to probe. It goes on to provide a format for organizing exit interview findings, and offers ten tips for attracting and retaining employees.

Recommendations: Turnover is a tricky issue to address within many companies because each instance when a good employee leaves reflects back so directly on that person's manager. To overcome the resistance to this topic that will inevitably emerge when you bring it up with your peers, you should develop an action plan that proceeds in three steps:

1. **Use the information provided in this Chapter to let your peers know just how widespread – and costly – the turnover problem is, not just in your company, but nation-wide. Your objective here is NOT to cast blame or draw comparisons within your own group, but to raise consciousness about the problem in general. Let the shock value of the numbers do that for you. And use all means at**

your disposal to pound the following statistic home with anyone who will listen:

2. If you don't already have one, institute an exit interview procedure IMMEDIATELY within your company or department, using the guidelines provided in this Chapter. If you do have an exit interview process, review the interview results, protecting the identities of the former employees involved by abstracting the information. What you are looking for are patterns or themes that can be addressed by the management group.

3. Once you've identified the causes of turnover within your department or company, make it your business to eradicate them.

Chapter Four –
Hiring Blunders We All Have Made

Synopsis: **Chapter Four** lists "10.5" hiring blunders that Hiring Managers should avoid like a bathtub full of spiders. Here are the headlines:

1: **Lowering Our Hiring Standards Because We're Under Pressure**

2: **Making an Offer to a Candidate After the First Interview**

3: **Making Hiring Decisions Too Much by Gut and Not Enough by Systems and Metrics**

4: **Qualifying on "Can Do's" to the Exclusion of "Will Do's"**

5: **Giving Up Too Easily on Reference Checks**

6: **Blowing the Interview through Lack of Preparation**

7: **Ignoring the Fact that Time Kills all Deals**

8: **Hiring People According to the Law of 10's Rather than for their Strengths**

9: **Talking too Much and Listening Too Little During Interviews**

10: **Getting Surprised at Offer Time**

10.5: **Failing to Keep Your Hiring Pipeline Full**

Key Points: While avoiding all of these Hiring Blunders is important, some take precedence because their toxins are so severe. Watch out in particular for these five:

❖ **# 7 – Time Kills All Deals -- Because you'll lose the best Candidates.**

◈ **# 2 – Making an Offer After the First Interview -- Because you're hiring a first impression, not a real person.**

◈ **# 4 – Qualifying on "Can-Do's" to the Exclusion of "Will-Do's" – Just because the candidate has the Skill, doesn't mean he or she has the Will, to do the job.**

◈ **# 10 – Getting Surprised at Offer Time – Because failure to ask the probing questions will inevitably come back to bite you.**

◈ **# 10.5 – Failing to Keep Your Hiring Pipeline Full – Because if you never get ahead of the curve, you'll always be behind it.**

Recommendations: In general, use the instructions, guidelines and pointers provided with each blunder to prevent it from happening to you. But take these two actions before you do anything else:

1. **Take a hard look at how long it currently takes for your company or department to move from first face-to-face interview to offer. Reorganize the process so it happens within two weeks.**

2. **Make it a requirement that no one can be hired (not even your nephew) after only one interview. Adopt the three-interview, ten-step hiring process put forth in Chapter Six.**

Chapter Five – Unleashing the Power of Personality

Synopsis: **Chapter Five** addresses the issue of personality, and introduces personality measurement as a useful tool in gauging the Soft Skills of the people we interview. In specific, it shows how the **DISC** approach to personality mapping can be used as a selection aid and management tool. It begins with these definitions:

$$D = \underline{D}ominance$$
$$I = \underline{I}nfluence$$
$$S = \underline{S}teadiness$$
$$C = \underline{C}ompliance.$$

It then goes on to show how people behave in predictable patterns, and how these patterns in turn either are a strong match to certain job roles or are not. DISC theory has been put into practice as a personality mapping instrument called the DISC Personality Survey. This Survey allows Hiring Managers to accomplish three objectives:

1. **To assess the strengths and weaknesses of the match between candidate or employee personality styles and specific job roles;**

2. **To develop benchmarks from the personality maps of top performers to aid in the identification of other potential top producers; and,**

3. **To identify and predict conflicts in personality styles that signify stress on the job.**

Key Points: Using a tool like the DISC Personality Survey gives Hiring Managers a definite edge over those who don't, in that it:

1. **Adds to their insights about a candidate's success factors;**

2. **Helps them configure and build more cohesive teams;**

3. **Enhances their day-to-day communications with staff;**

4. **Pinpoints potential trouble spots in making task assignments;**

5. **Serves as a guide in motivating individual staff members; and,**

6. **Hastens the "getting to know you" process with new hires.**

One of the more compelling features of the DISC Personality Survey and the theory that goes with it is that it can be used to empower Managers and team members to develop a more nonjudgmental view of the personality styles of other members of the team. The mantra is "Different is Different," and the meaning is that each person's style has an important contribution to make to the overall enterprise.

Recommendations: Personality assessment systems like the DISC Survey have an important role to play in helping you make informed hiring and management decisions. They should be implemented in companies of all sizes. Here are the first steps:

1. **Contact me and arrange to take the full DISC Personality Survey on line. You'll find that the cost is modest, the Survey is easy to use, and the feedback is immediate. We'll go over the results and discuss ways that the DISC Surveys can be applied to your company's hiring and management practices.**

2. **Implement the DISC Survey in your company or department: for hiring, for establishing performance benchmarks and to help you manage, develop and retain your staff.**

Chapter Six –
Hiring Winners

Synopsis: Chapter Six delivers on the promise made in Chapter Two, by laying out a practical, detailed, ten-step hiring process that has been specifically designed to achieve a balance in the way it considers Hard and Soft Skills. This hiring process is also configured to avoid the Hiring Blunders that are documented in Chapter Four. Each of the ten steps includes pointers, checklists, rules of thumb, guidelines, scripted phrases or interviewing tips to help you along your way.

Key Points: This is a proven process for recruiting and hiring that works. It's methodical enough to provide you with the essential verifiers and cross-checks, and is salesy and moves quickly enough to maintain the interest of your Candidates. It contains all of the tools you need to attract, interview, evaluate, select and hire the best Candidates while minimizing the effects of counter offers and other last-minute surprises.

Recommendations: Start at the top of the Chapter and follow the steps in order. To prepare, assemble the tools and facilities you'll need first, including:

❑ **Unique Selling Proposition – Company**

❑ **USP: Department and Opportunity**

❑ **Internal Job Posting & Referral Bonus**

❑ **Revised Recruitment Ads**

❑ **Phone Screen Voicemail Recording**

❑ **Open House or Discovery Night Logistics**

❑ **DISC Personality Survey & Benchmarks**

❑ **Prospective Candidate Rating Sheet**

❑ **Pre-Hire Paperwork**

Next, clear the decks. Focus on:

❑ **Overall Hiring Process Timing (Two Weeks)**

❑ **Receptionist Procedure re: Walk-Ins**

- [ ] Coordination: H/R, Other Departments
- [ ] Schedules of Key Staff & Decision-Makers
- [ ] Greeting Process for Candidates

Then, follow the ten Hiring Steps and accomplish the hire.

Chapter Seven --
Your Company's Real Wealth

Synopsis: **Chapter Seven** begins by stating that modern corporate wealth is now based on the knowledge of its employees. It uses Tom Peter's analogy of the eclipse of General Motors by Microsoft in the stock market as a centerpiece for the forty-year transformation that brought this new definition of wealth into being.

Key Points: The Chapter goes on to present eight actions that Hiring Managers can take to add stability to their employee base and build company wealth. Here are the highlights:

1. **Using the "Different is Different" Concept to Make Players into Winners.** How to draw upon DISC theory to reclaim the contributions of those on your team who may not be as flashy as your top performers, but are just as important.

2. **Training to Retain So You Don't Have to Replace and Re-Train.** Elements of a low-cost training plan that adds variety and growth to the working life of your staff.

3. **Fostering Teamwork that Works.** A primer on the characteristics and dynamics of building synergetic teams.

4. **Becoming a Guerilla Inspector.** Getting closer to your staff so you can find out what's really going on.

5. **Using the Sandwich Method for Constructive Feedback.** Three easy steps for packaging bad news so that your employees can actually hear it.

6. **Implementing Informal Reviews.** An important turnover-fighter that helps anchor your employees. Introduces the Interim Assessment Form.

7. **Reselling the Mission by Revisiting your USP's.** A lighthearted way to rewire your team to your objectives by creating a forum where they can resell themselves.

8. Hiring Right. The most important idea of all, it's Your Most Important Job.

Recommendations: You get to pick and choose which of these are the most apt for your situation. Based on their potential for stabilizing your organization, however, you might want to consider attacking these three choices first:

◈ **# 6 – Informal Reviews -- Because they go directly after an important cause of turnover.**

◈ **# 1 – Different is Different -- Because it helps bind your team together and enlists its members as your allies.**

◈ **# 2 – Training to Retain -- Because it will have a direct, positive and personal impact on your employees.**

<u>Chapter</u> <u>Eight</u> --
The <u>Proof</u> <u>is</u> <u>in</u> <u>the</u> <u>Doing</u>

That is my summary and these are my recommendations. The tools are here and the techniques have been presented -- the rest is up to you. Best of luck as you work on one of the most important competitive challenges in business and **Your Most Important Job** – attracting, recruiting, hiring and retaining great people for your company.

Thanks for your time and attention. Let me know how you're doing and how I can be of help.

Acknowledgements

No matter whose name is on the cover, a book like this one is always a collaborative effort, in the sense that a portion of what is presented was learned in association with others.

In that context, there are hundreds of people I could thank, and hopefully you all know that your contributions are valued. I would particularly like to thank the following people who worked closely with me during my years at Dunhill Staffing Systems, Inc. -- Rich De Santis, Jean Henninger, Tom Esposito, Rita Ingrassia, Phil Caparotta, Lynne Stewart, Pete Erbe, Karen Seketa, Bob Martineau, Ralph Daino, Mark Brunkhorst and John Formica.

Special thanks as well go to my good friend and associate, Rick Kean, who has been my logic coordinator and editorial consultant during this project. Rick continues to be one of the finest trainers in the search and staffing industry today.

About the Author

Daniel Abramson, CTS, is President and Founder of **StaffDynamics**, and has been focused on workforce performance issues and raising the bar for over 25 years. Prior to **StaffDynamics**, he was President of  an international search and staffing firm with over 100 locations. Under his leadership, revenues nearly tripled, and profits increased almost nine-fold.

Daniel has a keen under-standding of today's business culture as it relates to planning, re-engineering and leveraging change. His unique blend of hands-on management skills, and his knowledge of organizational styles and structures and human capital development, enables him to provide strategic services through consulting, speaking, coaching and content-rich training sessions. During his career, Daniel has developed unique and effective systems that increase human potential, help move from attitude into action, and assist organizations and individuals in redefining performance standards.

Daniel earned his Bachelor's degree in Marketing and has MBA credits. He is a certified instructor of Xerox Professional Selling Skills and DISC personality assessments, and has completed the Dale Carnegie program. In addition, he is a member of the National Speakers Association, and the National Association of Training and Development. He lives in the Washington, DC area with his wife, two daughters, and a bevy of pets.